Brewing, Ballet and Bedpans
The Memoirs of Elizabeth Coxon-Taylor

The Taylor Family
Elizabeth bottom right with the plaits

Produced in association with

Bound Biographies

21 Heyford Park House, Heyford Park, Bicester, Oxon OX25 5HD
www.boundbiographies.com

Dedication

To the whole family

Life is a hard fight, a struggle, a wrestling with the principle of evil, hand to hand, foot to foot. Every inch of the way is disputed. The night is given to us to take breath and to pray, to drink deep at the fountain of power; the day to use the strength which has been given us, to go forth to work with it till the evening.

Florence Nightingale

Take, O Lord, and receive all my liberty, my memory, my understanding and all my will, all that I have and possess. Thou hast given them to me; to Thee, O Lord, I restore them; all things are Thine, dispose of them according to Thy will. Give me Thy love and Thy grace, for this is enough for me.

Saint Ignatius Loyola, 1491-1556

Upon thy bended knees, thank God for work –
Work – once man's penance, now his high reward!
For work to do, and strength to do the work,
We thank Thee, Lord.

John Oxenham, 1858-1941

Acknowledgements

I would like to express my gratitude to many friends who have helped me with this book. Mike and Sally at *Bound Biographies* have stood by me for several years as I dithered and finally decided to proceed before I got too old. My neighbours Mick and Thelma Brooks have also given magnificent help to complete the task.

I must also pay tribute to my kind tutors at West Kent College who conducted many sessions instructing me in the intricacies of word-processing.

My final thanks must go to my cousin Daphne Coyne for her encouragement and wise advice throughout the project – this book would not have been possible without her tremendous support.

Note: The author is working on a family tree via the internet and records supplied by Tim Faulkner whose grandfather Geoffrey Coxon had researched his family back in the Saxon and Norman times. Anyone wishing for a copy, please contact the author.

Contents

Illustrations Index

Foreword

Reading this Memoir by my friend Elizabeth one may be forgiven for wondering how one person could cram so many – and such varied – experiences into one life.

Two qualities shine out from these pages. The first is Elizabeth's honesty – about herself, her struggles, her fears, her setbacks, as well as her joys and victories. The second is her love – for her own family and for the 'adopted' family of her much-loved and sorely-missed husband Ted. Indeed, writing this Memoir has been for Elizabeth quite literally a labour of love.

St John tells us that, "Perfect love drives away fear." Elizabeth's story is not only fascinating but ultimately inspiring, as she traces her, often quite difficult, journey away from the household of fear (in Henry Nouwen's memorable phrase) and into the household of love.

Hugh Williams
Yalding, Kent
15th March 2004

In the Beginning

Engraved on the window in a semi circle at Grandpa's solicitor's office in Burton-on-Trent was the name 'Ormsby Taylor' – his home was previously Peel House, a short distance away, originally the home of Sir Robert Peel who began the 'Peelers' or Police Force. When, as a child, I visited Grandma, she lived in Ashby Road – a tall house with stone steps down to the kitchen, and a sitting room with a warm gas-fire and a huge picture of two lions. My grandparents lived with Aunt Audrey, their only unmarried daughter, who taught music. At the end of term, concerts were held in the music room and the long suffering parents arrived to hear the little darlings perform.

Peel House

Grandmother Maria Taylor née Carter Wigg married Ormsby
Taylor at St Alkmonton Church Derby on September 9th 1887

My cousin John, aged three or four, somehow got in – having fingered the piano when no one was about. The 'Jolly Farmer' and other pieces were performed one after the other. At one point one child got stuck and kept going back to the beginning – John, having been told off many times, piped up in the middle of the other child's piano piece, "That will do Kathleen," to the consternation of the child's mother, and prompt banishment of my cousin from the room.

His mother Nancy, the second daughter, married Tudor Owen, a clergyman. Her younger sister Olive was Harry Prince's wife – he was later a bank manager at Broadway in the Cotswolds. My mother was the eldest in the family, marrying Fred Coxon, head brewer at *Bass* brewery.

The one son, my Uncle Roland Taylor, was in the First World War where he met my Aunt Edythe in Cairo. Their son Richard died in the 1990s, Richard's father also a solicitor having been Mayor of Wembley latterly.

Within five years of my father's death in 1927, all the sisters and my grandmother lost their husbands, so we had much time together with a number of great aunts, indeed, a surfeit of aunts. Aunt Audrey, my mother's youngest sister, was married later in life and lived in a beautiful old farmhouse amidst cherry orchards in Charing, Kent. Here the blossom was a wonderful sight when I got away from the bombing of Canterbury, where I worked as a nurse in the war.

Our Great Aunts Georgie, Lizzie and May lived in Balham. They seemed to have the blinds down permanently, and sat in the front pew in church. When they died, the vicar felt the pillars of the church had collapsed – so straight did they sit during the services. Great Aunt Emily lived in Hammersmith and had breakfast at 4.30

am. When I was a dancing student she brought me a delicious boiled egg, bread and butter.

On my father's side I did not have so many aunts, but Grandpa had a large house in Horninglow, later used for Council Offices in Burton. Most of the Coxons are buried in the church nearby.

My father and mother both came from well established families in the Midlands, meeting frequently at the local 'Barnstormers' – amateur dramatic shows much appreciated before cinema and television, as my parents sang well.

Barnstormers – Father top left next to Mother
Front row: centre Roland Taylor with his sister Nancy on his left

When my grandfather aged, he lost his memory, repeating, "What day is it my dear?" every few minutes as we sat by a very hot gas fire in the morning room at Ashby Road. Granny was a wonderful cook, and the smell of her raspberry buns was unforgettable as we entered the house on a cold afternoon. The bridge parties were a regular feature, and she cut the daintiest plates of bread and butter. The story my mother told me was of her newly engaged fiancé placing two bottles of *Bass* beer in the middle of the tea table, unseen by my grandmother, which shocked her prim and proper bridge-playing guests!

Paternal Grandmother

Daddy's father and grandfather had both been Mayor of Burton. My father did brilliantly at Shrewsbury with his elder brother, Arthur, later a Canon of Litchfield Cathedral. Daddy won a scholarship to Caius College Cambridge, but was prevented from taking it up because he caught rheumatic fever. He subsequently worked for Lord Burton at the brewery, where his scientific knowledge was of immense value. Lord Nuffield, who founded *Morris Motors*, used to mend Uncle Arthur's bicycle when Arthur was at St John's College, Oxford. He joked that if you called out "John", half the windows of the college would open. I remember him telling me that marmalade was known as 'squidge in the pot'.

Great-Grandfather,
Mayor of Burton

My father, Fred, his brother Arthur,
and their parents (my grandparents)

A first class cricketer, my father took his team abroad, and in England he had the job of selling hops in Kent where local families still have similar connections today. One short fellow cricketer who looked up to Daddy said, "You must have been well manured, Mr Coxon, when you was young!!" My father was six foot six inches tall.

My mother wrote, and had published, three charming little songs, later broadcast on the new 'wireless' which we enjoyed at family get-togethers. As children we were told, "If people are kind enough to ask you to perform, then you must do it." How my poor cousins John and Daphne hated it. With a very bad grace we all dragged out the poems and music pieces of last term as we bored our mothers' elderly visitors. All our aunts and uncles had been brought up to 'entertain' so it was no hardship for that generation.

A precious cartoon of my tall father as a cricketer.

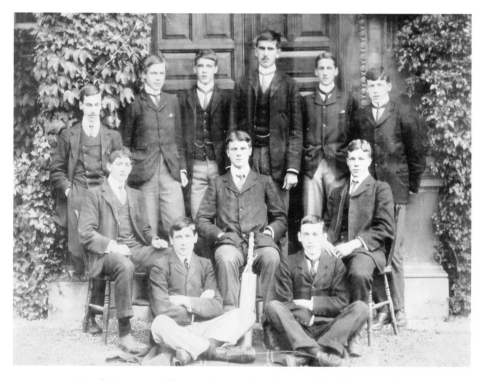

Fred Coxon at Shrewsbury – back row third from right

The wedding photographs portray my mother's sisters' hats at strange angles. They were all too small, and these attractive young ladies were forced to drag them onto their heads at what appear to be most peculiar positions.

My parents' wedding, showing the odd angles of my aunts' hats!

My parents' wedding at Peel House,
next to the Burton Football Ground

My mother had trained at the Guildhall School of Music in London – she had a beautiful mezzo soprano voice, and was much in demand at local charity concerts. One day the local 'aristocracy' invited her to sing, and Nancy came along to keep her company. Their clothes were laid out by a maid in the magnificent bedroom, and my mother hoped their evening dresses would meet the situation. To their amazement they went down to dinner to see their three hostesses – one in full evening dress with tiara, the second in afternoon 'tea gown', and the third in a coat and skirt and a 'pork pie' hat. The diversity of clothing was easily explained, "So that none of the villagers at the concert would feel uncomfortable wearing the wrong type of dress."

There was not much education provided for the girls in the family – a series of governesses and time at the Litchfield School. By then the family had settled at *Erisbeg*, a huge house at Barton-under-Needwood (now an old people's home), near the station for Grandpa to get to Burton easily.

Grandfather's brother had settled in Derby as a Medical Consultant. One day a nurse came to him. "Doctor Taylor," she said, "a rat has eaten off half a baby's ear."

One day Grandfather travelled by train after a celebratory dinner with his local football team. One was a well-known town councillor who was overcome by sleep and lent back in the carriage with his ticket in his pocket in full view of his colleagues. Snatching it quickly from the overweight gentleman's pocket, his friend heard the ticket collector approaching, and much searching for tickets took place. "It will not look good if you have not got a ticket," said one gentleman to another. "What shall I do?" said the robust councillor.

"You'd better get under the seat and we'll put our legs over you," was the reply.

"Oh," said the ticket collector, "Eleven tickets, and only ten gentlemen."

"He prefers to travel that way," was the reply!

My father was working such long hours that I do not remember seeing much of him, but I recall that he took me blackberry picking, and helped me make a garden with multicolour flowers grown from seed. Granny had given us raspberry canes, and we also kept fowls. One night my mother threw up the bedroom window, and discovered that a fox had finished off our cherished chickens. There was one consolation from this tragic event, as the hen house proved a splendid committee room for those of us involved in Missions to Seamen – we were given some sort of uniform we wore for 'best' when aged seven.

Richard Taylor

My other cousin, Richard Taylor, Uncle Roland's son, came to join us for plays. I made him wear my Brownie uniform when he had to appear as an earwig. Later he was to produce the film of *Chitty Chitty Bang Bang,* and visited Africa to make films. The car in Chitty was filmed on Beachy Head, and as it took off into the sky, Richard had to create the hill on top of the cliffs.

One night we were got out of bed to see a huge warehouse on fire in the Derby Road. I suppose my parents were interested and couldn't leave me alone in the house.

Pom Sechiari, a very dear friend, looked after me when I was three because my mother gave singing lessons, was Enrolling Member of the Mothers' Union, and also secretary of the RSPCA, so she had a very busy life.

My father adored birds and went down every year to West Dean near Chichester, staying with the Sechiari family who lived at Lodge Hill, opposite Bow Hill near Chilgrove. One day he found a nightingale's nest, having heard it sing, and he walked round that point in ever increasing circles. My mother said he was like a schoolboy throwing his cap in the air.

Old Shrewsbury records I have show how successful my father was at school – both academically and at sport, especially cricket and football.

At Christmas we were taken to the Barke's huge house near Stoke-on-Trent – another set of relations on my father's side. Later Reginald was to work with Lawrence of Arabia in Mesopotamia and his son was, until recently, in charge of land belonging to Salisbury Cathedral.

A school in Staffordshire meant that my accent, when returning home, required constant correction. It had somewhat changed years later when doing programmes on Radio Kent and Radio Sussex after my husband died (before his mammoth 47th London to

Brighton motorcycle ride), and on the 'Lift up Your Hearts' programmes.

I think I was born in the local nursing home. One of my first memories is of being taken to see my cousin Daphne Coyne, née Owen, who was 'on show' in the maternity room; I recall seeing my little red headed, red faced relative in her cot. She and her brother John spent much of their childhood at Marchington Vicarage which I and my parents visited fairly frequently, having been collected at the village station (next stop was Uttoxeter) in the pony and trap. Later we acquired a bull-nosed *Morris Cowley*. How frightening those steep hills to Burton were, and my father refused to drive – he disliked driving – so it was left to my mother. On one occasion, when driving to Derby, the radiator burst as we were going up hill and my mother's feet got soaked.

Marchington Vicarage

Various of Elizabeth as a baby, with Barbara Stretton-Burgis (wearing glasses), her mother, my mother and Nancy Owen

When we still lived at White Ley, Branston, my mother gave me a little bowl to wash my dolls clothes out in the garden near some wonderful smelling red roses. On other days I made 'mud pies' with the dark earth and water. Oh how lovely the vicarage garden was – drenched with snowdrops in the fields, which Aunt Nancy sent to us by post in cardboard boxes each year, then primroses and deep blue grape hyacinths in the 'spinney'. We had tea under the spreading copper beech tree, and there were lovely hedges where we made endless 'houses', ready for my next visit from Burton – if I wasn't too home sick and had to be fetched home!

Strange French men used to come and stay as PGs (paying guests) as my aunt and uncle, like everyone else in the 1920s, were always short of money. When my uncle died suddenly, his widow had £200 to live on and educate two children. She loved producing village plays and everything dramatic.

Four generations – Great Grandmother Wigg,
Grandmother, Mother and Elizabeth

At the age of four I was taken to the dentist for three stoppings, and afterwards paid the regular post-dental visit to *Boots* or the confectioners *Bailey* to be given ice cream or a meringue. Granny would take me to the pictures. How we loved Charlie Chaplin – especially *Gold Rush* with the house teetering on the mountain's edge.

My father, as town councillor, visited the workhouse regularly. He and my mother would sing to the residents, and I had to dance there at the age of five. When my mother obtained the Duchess of Portland's interest in the local RSPCA, I had to present a huge bouquet of pink carnations – she gave me one, and Daddy collected me off the stage before I burst into tears. Another great thrill was the 'cat's whiskers' wireless set and straining to hear the first notes of the 'radio' – years later we had a similar experience watching my colleagues performing at the Alexander Palace for the first dancing show on television, when I was a student of dance and drama.

It was a joy to play 'theatre' with puppets and cardboard scenery in rooms lighted by gas mantles and cared for by my dearest Pom Sechiari. She told me, just before her death, that she had come to help my mother when I was three, when my "nose was running and my drawers were hanging down."

Great Uncle Seymour, a well-known physician, lived in Wembley, and his daughter Felicia lived with him. She had been presented to King George and Queen Mary, and had an amusing story of the occasion, which I had better not relate for reasons of diplomacy! Great Uncle Seymour used to make me skip backwards to open my shoulders. Felicia ended her days caring for John Buchan's widow in Berkshire.

Aunt Dora Buckley was another of Father's cousins. Her brother was managing director of *Barclays Bank* in London, and she herself became a surgeon in her forties. Staying with her in Wimpole Street was so useful when I had appointments in London. My mother's grandfather was also a London Doctor and used to take her in a pony and trap when visiting patients in Kensington.

When Florence Nightingale was in Scutari, she sent for Taylor's book on medicine – another doctor relative. She wrote, "I solemnly pledge myself before God and in presence of the assembly to pass my life in purity. I will abstain from whatever is deleterious and mischievous… I will do all in my power to elevate the standard of my profession… with loyalty I will endeavour to aid the physician in his work and devote myself to the welfare of those committed to my care." (*Hope for Today*, Grosvenor Books.)

As a child I used to go up to Grandpa's bedroom where a saucepan containing a few senna pods would be stewing on a small gas ring in the bedroom, to 'keep him regular'! Another great Aunt – Florence I believe – was the first woman to climb the Matterhorn mountain in Switzerland. My parents loved Switzerland; Daddy went in the summer to see the beauty of wild flowers, and Mummy went skiing with a party of friends. I was sometimes left with Mrs Auden (the poet's mother), and the sister of W H Auden came regularly to stay with us. She was an artist and had a very bothersome stammer.

When the parents of Daphne and John were away, the children stayed at school as boarders, telling their friends, "Daddy and Mummy are on their honeymoon" – so nice for the local vicar's reputation! One child asked them, "Haven't you got a Granny for the rough?" Grandmothers were in great demand then, as they are now.

Woolworth's did not sell anything over 6d, so it was a treat to visit Burton shops. In 1954 it hadn't changed much. One day I was trying on my mother's hats at the end of her bed and toppled over trying to see myself in the mirror. The broken collarbone never bothered me later in life.

In order to have some time by the sea, my father bought a bungalow at East Wittering to which we could escape from the Midlands. Oil lamps lit it, and cooking was carried out by the same method (*Valor perfection*). It had four double bedrooms, and an outside loo emptied weekly by a gentleman who came at night for the *Elsan*. When my father died suddenly in 1927, my mother used the bungalow to take paying guests, often children whose parents were abroad. During World War II it was occupied by the army and subsequently demolished. We had exciting fancy headdress parties and were only about 50 yards from the beach. I learnt horse riding, falling off on my first effort on wet sand.

Left: Mrs Auden, the poet's mother
Right: my godmother left front, behind her Mr & Mrs Auden, Grandpa standing in the back, Pom Sechiari in front, my mother to her left, me, and to my left Ruth Auden

Wittering days, Elizabeth and friends

Our Burton house was next to a large field belonging to a much bigger home of Mrs Graham, an old lady who let it out for an annual fair to which gypsies came; I found them quite frightening when they called to me when I was playing in the garden. I had four imaginary friends who lived in the ex-hen house – Doubler, Cherry, Frear and Daney, and talked endlessly to them, as an only child can.

On May 1st the gypsies visited us with a flower covered maypole and the inevitable pegs. If we gave them food they chalked a message on our gatepost as a sign to their friends that we were a 'soft touch' – a common sign in the 1920s. Years later my cousin was still feeding their descendants at the vicarage on Boxing Days in the 1980s.

Nearby lived the Shread family whom I longed to mix with – they were sophisticated and had a well-known local grocer's store. Stanley had a birthday on the same day as mine. Our parents had written in to *Children's Hour* to have our birthdays announced on the wireless, but the 'uncles' and 'aunts', as we called the announcers, mixed the messages – it should have been, "Stanley Shread, look for your present in the grandfather clock, and Elizabeth Coxon, yours is in the cupboard under the stairs." The result was, "Elizabeth Coxon, look in the grandfather's clock (which we did not possess)."

On my fifth birthday I was given cornflakes for tea with sugar on. I thought it was very 'infra dig' – common! Our nursery school was quite near, but when I went to the kindergarten attached to Burton High School, the elastic in my pants gave way and I had to stand by the sand tray with the toys until rescued by the mistress and taken home on the first day.

Sir Edwin Burgis, another uncle on my father's side, was appointed to the Northern Circuit as a Judge during the Second World War. We stayed with him in Barlastone and he gave me some lovely *Liberty* material, later to be made into a dress. He had sentenced a conscientious objector who then waited for him at Stafford station and stabbed him. Uncle survived and later received a knighthood!

Clothes meant much to us, whether Bo Peep costumes or red velvet party dresses with white collars. We had dancing classes on Saturday morning in a very cold hall at Burton, wearing our bronze 'pumps' (dancing shoes with elastic straps). A fire made little difference, and the teacher's hands seemed frozen as she tried to steer us round the room for a foxtrot or to prepare us for the 'show'. This was held at the town hall, after hours of toil from my mother and Pom to make me like a violet (somewhat unsuccessfully). The only time I felt happy was in the Polka (many years later I was high kicking in the back row of the chorus in Rosemarie – so it must have had some use).

Uncle Edwin Burgis

We were never allowed to believe we were anything but plain children. If we fussed about our appearance, Grannie would say, "No one is going to stop the carriage to look at you, my girl." My cousin Vivien had a beautiful mother. On one occasion Nanny took him with her to buy a new hat. As she tried on hats above a somewhat ordinary face, Vivien remarked, "Nanny it's the face wot's the matter."

Elizabeth as a young girl in Burton-on-Trent
Arthur Coxon (my uncle) and Geoffrey Coxon
(half brother to my father)

The Burgis family lived near the Wedgwood family in Barlastone. My Uncle Arthur meanwhile lived in Tunstall in the Potteries, and his parishioners were the factory workers. There were 17,000 in his parish, and there was immense poverty in the 1920s. My mother was given half a lamb, which we brought back from Scotland, with heather honey. Needless to say our case was filled with honey-covered leg of lamb when we arrived at the vicarage. I burst into tears seeing the terrible condition of the children in the streets, especially as we had just had such a splendid holiday. Nigel, my cousin and a few years younger, was at home, and continued the family tradition of being educated at Shrewsbury. Later his son also went there and then to Cambridge.

Nigel Coxon (centre)

Rev Arthur Coxon used to emphasise that ministers should visit, visit, visit. On one very cold day he went to the house of one of his parishioners. The room was full – the fire was blazing, the meal prepared, which went on and on, with true Midland's hospitality. Suddenly a some-what adenoidal child shouted, "Moother we've forgotten the moofins," and a huge plate of muffins was quickly produced. My uncle, for politeness' sake, had to partake of yet another tea bun. For many years the family joke was to repeat this child's remark when we were replete after Christmas festivities.

The window in St Peter's Walsall depicts Christ giving Communion; the face was modelled on Great Uncle Charlie (McCreery), who was later made a Prebendary. He was a Canon at Litchfield Cathedral and Walsall, another poverty stricken town with coal mines all around. (I noticed that the pavements had begun to collapse in the '80s on my last visit.) When we visited on a boat trip on Loch Lomand, he demanded that "Elizabeth Ann (as my great grandmother was called) must see the Trossachs." He had one baked apple every day for breakfast.

The Christmas children's party for the parish was again heart rending. The last time I saw British children running in the streets was in 1937 in Chelsea when I taught children dancing in Battersea – the Walsall visit was in the '20s. The spire at my Uncle Arthur's church fell down, and fortunately no one was injured in Tunstall, but I realised how wise it was to take our Pembury Church spire down in our village in the 1980s.

Our garden in Burton had my father's favourite flowers – deep blue cornflowers, phlox and many coloured lupins. A privet hedge separated us from the main Branston Road, and I was taken for walks to the *Branston* pickle factory which had a seemingly endless wall round the works. Houses were sold for £100 to the workers after the First World War – very nice looking they were.

Living near the *Crosse and Blackwell* factory, I was taken to visit old Mrs Blackwell, who lived near the tram stop. She sat clothed rather like Queen Victoria, in a black high-necked full-skirted dress of rustling silk, and she gave me a lovely pot of *C&B* marmalade. All the orange peel had been cut in the shape of little fish, and the whole result was of tiny goldfish swimming in a jam-jar full of orange jelly.

Another regular visitor was Aunt Bessie Chamberlain MBE (for her services to Guiding). We kept in touch for many years, but she was quite a strong character.

On some train journeys to London we saw boards in the fields advertising *Carter's Little Liver Pills,* but what interested us was the number of miles to London so that we could calculate how long it would be before we arrived at St Pancras station. Granny used *Carter's* pills and years later I made friends with the widow of *Beecham's* pills, who drove me, in 1966, at 100 mph in Kent in an open sports car on the A2 near Maidstone – I was terrified.

Sundays were times of church-going. I remember snuggling up against my mother's fur collar during the sermon. It was fashionable for our friends to have fox furs (which had intriguing fastening for little fingers), and cloche hats were the rage in the '20s and '30s – they come back into fashion periodically.

One of the First World War planes had come down in a field in Branston, and my mother recalled the Zeppelins coming to Burton. When all the street lights were on, people threw stones up to the lamps as, despite there being no black out, there was immense panic. I also remember in the thirties the R10I Zeppelin drifting over before it caught fire.

On fine nights the dining room table would be taken into the garden and we children would literally sleep on top of it out under the stars in August, watching them shooting across the sky. Every time I dropped off to sleep my cousins would shout out, "There's another one."

As I made a rice pudding recently, I remembered our Brownie 1st Class exam to make up a brown paper parcel with string (*Sellotape* had not been invented), make a rice pudding, and light a fire in our home with sticks, paper and matches. When we became Guides and were inspected by HM the Queen Mother at Hatfield House, somehow my nametape 'Second Company Christ's Hospital' had not been sewn on my shoulder. My whole day was ruined by my worry – as if anyone among hundreds of Girl Guides would have noticed. The stress of always doing the right thing was beginning to tell – the fear of letting the school down.

This fear was inherited from my time at the Girls' High School at Burton-on-Trent, to which we travelled daily by tram. Some very rough children attacked me, pulled my mackintosh off, and subsequently left it on the top of the tram.

Next day it was held up at assembly in front of the whole school – hundreds of girls. My shame at having to claim it was compounded because it was a green mackintosh with a hood, and no one else wore such a little red riding hood garment. I was mortified, having to collect it as mine – so childish, but my mother obviously felt it would protect me in the rain.

Years later I watched little boys from a similar background, but at Portsmouth Harbour, diving for pennies in the frightful mud as the sea came in, and I realised how fortunate my life had been. Henry Drummond (1851-97) wrote, "The mind of Christ is to be learned in the family. Strength of character may be acquired at work but beauty of character is learned at home. There the affections are trained. Mothers make most of the stones for the buildings of the City of God, and all the best of them are made by mothers."

A bedtime drink my father favoured was 'Pobs' – a name I met in another book recently, made of bread, milk and sugar – a splendid night cap I've often used when worried at bedtime.

When we had whooping cough we were sent out on to the road menders' site to bend over their buckets of steaming tar – a cheap inhalation. Measles time meant a sheet hung over the bedroom door to supposedly prevent the rest of the family catching it. Needless to say they did, and were much worse than me.

If you had astigmatism, you were made to sit in front of a wooden contraption for a long time (15 mins) looking at pictures until they overlapped in your vision. At the age of 18 I was sitting again for appearance purposes – I had knock knees (my dancing teacher said), so had to sit each day for 30 minutes with my ankles strapped together and cushions in the middle of my knees – agony – whilst studying the theory of Greek dancing.

Saturday mornings at the age of five onwards were devoted to French lessons with Joy Frowen, whose father, a much-loved GP, delivered my mother. Having no children, Joy and her husband were very generous, one year making me an exquisite wardrobe of doll's clothes, including skiing and skating outfits in a tiny wardrobe with hangers. Another year it was a doll's bed, with a light fixed over the head attached to a battery switch. The beautiful crimson satin eiderdown accompanied the hem-stitched sheets – it was a wonderful Christmas gift.

"Penny or a Ticket," this was the cry as we waited for our tram after school at Burton-on-Trent High School. A term's supply of tickets could be exchanged daily, one-by-one, for a penny clutched by some of us, whilst bolder spirits did brisk business at the sweet shop opposite on our hot coins, having given us one of their tickets in return. One day, unexpectedly, Daddy appeared on the upstairs of our tram. How cross he was when I shouted "Oh Daddy," as any sign of 'showing off' was taboo.

My father started vomiting on Friday night. He had recently been made a town councillor (the only Conservative win North of the Trent). My mother rushed up and down stairs with clean pyjamas and sheets. I was sent to Granny's home. On Monday, Daddy was dead, July 19th 1927. The diagnosis was sleeping sickness. Some years ago I spoke to a doctor who said that there was a world epidemic of the disease that year. My father had been destined for a distinguished political career but sadly died aged 44.

After my father's death we moved to Shrewsbury where John, Daphne and I were sent to a PNEU (Parent's National Education Union) school – I was eight years old. It was a very long walk from St Giles vicarage each day, and we had an ex-First World War Sergeant to teach us drill. I remember that we could not afford the delicious buns for sale at a farthing (¼d) each at morning break.

Recently, whilst writing my memoirs, I had a dream – some senior personage was urging me to undertake an important engagement, and I replied that I could not do it, as I had my mother with me. I awoke to find my dear mother was no longer here, and that I was free to carry out my other duty – a throw-back to the day after my father's death when my Godfather took me, aged 8, on his lap saying, "Now you must look after your mother."

My parents were always keen members of the church, and my grandfather was instrumental in raising money for the local St Chad's church in Burton. My Uncle Geoffrey Coxon raised money for Sevenoaks Maternity Hospital many years later (1967). God must have guided the wife of one of my father's senior executives, who woke one morning after Daddy's death with the thought, "What is going to happen to the Coxon child?" John Gretton was our MP, Director of my father's firm *Bass Radcliffe and Gretton,* and also a Governor of Christ's Hospital. He presented me and enabled me to be educated there for eight years, so now I left the PNEU school after less than a year – John went to St Edmund's, Canterbury, and Daphne to St Margaret's, Bushey.

Lady Chapel at St Chad's Church, Burton-on-Trent

Meanwhile my visits to 208 Ashby Road, Burton continued on a regular basis. I remember the pretty pictures my grandmother made from flowers in the garden, placed behind a piece of glass and fastened round the edges with passé-patou, and also the rather ugly but much-loved rabbits she made us from scraps of material in her work bag.

If I could walk far enough we crossed the Ferry Bridge over the Trent. One winter the river froze and, dressed in long white leggings, I was allowed to slide on the ice. The disastrous state of my appearance, having fallen on the muddy melting ice, produced more work (no washing machines then, just the copper in the back kitchen).

In the summer the larder ceiling was peppered with corks – Granny's nettle beer had, as usual, exploded. It was delicious, made with nettles, yarrow and other wild herbs, and pretty potent. She said it gave you the, "Beg your pardon feeling" as we burped our way through lunch.

Colonel Reginald Barke (Uncle Reg)

My first homemade camera was made from a cigar box, a pillbox and other necessities outlined in the one of eight volumes of Arthur Mee's *Children's Encyclopaedia*. I was so proud to see the outline of our roof in the resulting photo. My cousin Daphne remembers the smell of *Lott's Bricks* and I was furious when my famous Uncle Colonel Reg Barke took over the whole box of bricks to build a brilliant model battleship, which stayed on the mantelpiece for days, much to my chagrin.

> An expert is one who knows the worst things that can happen and manages to avoid them.

School Years

Be ye steadfast, unmovable, always abounding in the
work of the Lord, for as much as ye know that your
labour is not in vain in the Lord.

I Corinthians 15:58

After my father's death I must have been banished from our house,
as I remember nothing of the upheaval, and staying with Granny I
remember strange wallpaper in the bedroom (reminiscent of the
Chinese bird wallpaper I saw many years later at Brighton Pavilion)
in my bedroom.

My mother got a job looking after Kingston House near Oxford,
which belonged to A E Strauss MP. He used it when he entertained
shooting parties, but Mother had never been taught to control a
large staff, and had much opposition from the butler. She used to
come home to the lovely Cotswold cottage we were given nearby, in
tears. People used to 'walk the hounds' for the Old Berks Hunt.
One day, one of these dogs escaped and helped himself to a leg of
lamb my mother had got for our weekend lunch. For many years
we saw the name 'A E Strauss' on the hoardings just outside
London Bridge Station – he was a well-known hop merchant.

Coming yet again to my rescue with her memories, Daphne has
urged me to write about my mother's sense of humour. Thrown
together as we were – an only child and a widow – I did not
appreciate my mother's enthusiasm, her zest for life, but also how

easily she was swayed by new ideas. One memory I have is of an invitation we had to join a clergyman and his wife from the Isle of Wight when they moved to South Africa.

Left: Winifred Coxon   Right: Winifred Coxon (with gauntlet gloves) with Mrs Weir on her right. Members of the WRVS during the war with the late Queen Mother at Bosham (the church is in the Bayeux Tapestry).

It was the time of the sales in the shops in London, and short of money as she was, she took me and bought masses of cheap clothes – evening dresses for the boat and other suitable outfits for South African society. I do remember her making an appointment with my Christ's Hospital Head, Miss Craig, who persuaded her that it would be more beneficial for me to stay at school for an extra year. All our carefully planned garments lay idle.

However, in her usual outgoing manner, my mother invited a neighbour of generous proportions to a party. My aunts, cousins and mother put on clothes for an evening sitting comfortably by the fire. Daphne retired for a long bath and could hear everything. Suddenly the front doorbell rang and Mrs Weir stood there, to my mother's horror, in full evening dress with diamante jewellery. Thinking quickly, my mother apologised saying that she and her sisters were just changing after going out to afternoon tea, and sat the visitor in the drawing room. There was then an almighty rush for the bedroom with all our South African-destined clothes. All the aunts put on whatever they could find of shoes and evening dresses etc; nothing fitted at all, but mother carried off the evening with dignity – so I am told.

John and Daphne were roped in to do plays. John, as Alfred who burnt the cakes, could remember no more of his part except, "I wish I could beat the Danes," with much prompting from me (having done it at school).

In order to pass the entrance exam for Christ's Hospital I had to walk about four miles, after the village school mistress had finished teaching at 4.00 pm. She coached me splendidly, otherwise I should never have had eight wonderful years' education at Christ's hospital.

We children had energetic games in the barn and garden. When I was on a Women's Institute Course in 1990, just after my husband's death, one of the tutors took me to see Kingston House as we were studying Victorian Architecture, and I saw our old home, *Little South Moor Farm*, rather gentrified after 70 years, but still beautiful. Incidentally, this is the village where Dr David Kelly committed suicide in 2003 – he was the expert whose death was investigated by the Hutton inquiry, which raised questions about the Iraq war and the BBC.

Mr Strauss had 3,000 acres on his estate – many were used to grow hops, which is how my father met him. The estate agent, Mr Tanner, lived in a beautiful 'New House' with tennis courts and beds of asters all round. Nearby, the hops were dried, and this was the first time hops were grown outside Kent, Herefordshire or Worcestershire.

Ladies living in big houses nearby sold fruit, grown on the estate, in a delightful tent. This was a completely new idea. Now fruit is sold throughout the country at the roadside.

I was sometimes allowed to help with the hoppers – the local villagers and gypsies were all involved. The smell of fresh hops is unforgettable, likewise the drying sheds. In the war I smelt it again when lying in bed after a hard day's nursing in the Kent and Canterbury Hospital – the smell wafted in from the local oast house as our bedroom windows were left open (before black out curtains were put in).

One day I found a snake in a beech wood nearby where I was sketching – a harmless grass snake but frightening nevertheless.

New House had a ha-ha, and I remember trying to learn hymns sitting on the wall and being told I was to have a new pink dress for a party. Mr and Mrs Tanner, the estate agent and his wife, were very kind to us, and my mother was an attractive asset at their parties. Their only son, Joe, a pilot, was killed in the war. Their fireplace had a metal backing with the words 'Nihil Desperandum' – I was thrilled as it was the motto of my house at Christ's Hospital. How we yelled at house hockey and netball matches, "Nihil Desperandum" – do not despair.

Kingston House

My mother's job at Kingston House was very stressful, organising the catering and running the huge house with staff, so she left and resorted to taking guests in our bungalow at East Wittering to make ends meet. We left Oxfordshire for Sussex, where we were inundated with visitors. School holidays were spent wherever my mother was working – it was not easy being the landlady's daughter. My mother had to give up her music, as money was short and life was tough.

Christ's Hospital had an unforgettable influence on my whole life and I am immensely grateful for my eight years education there. The discipline, the caring, the friendships made, and camaraderie is something I am proud to pass on as a Governor and to the boy being educated there whom I chose out of over 70 applicants. Lately, writing obituary notices for the school magazine, I looked at old speech day and sports day programmes, recalling some wonderful times.

We arrived at Hertford East station on our first day in September 1928 at the age of nine and were handed over to Miss Mossop, our Ward Matron (housemistress), who pointed to Margaret Wright and myself and said, "Now you two must be friends" – rather off-putting, as we had only just looked at one another. Margaret lived near the school – her father was often away as a Chaplain in the Missions to Seamen, and her Godmother was our Headmistress (which I did not know until a later date). I am pleased to record that indeed Margaret and I became lifelong friends.

Responsibility of day-to-day care laid with our 'School Mother', a girl in a senior form. In return we nine-year-olds had to clean our 'mother's' large black laced-up shoes and make her bed. We were taken into a small cupboard-like room where the sweets were locked away, and given our ration of four sweets three times a week. This room led off from the main ward day room, as did the music practice room where the piano was played each night for prayers.

The school song of seven verses in Latin was drummed into us by half term, by our long-suffering school mother, and now, 75 years later, we belt it out on Speech Day each year for the Lord Mayor's enjoyment! Our verse of Artes Palaestrae, bidding the girls to excel in the arts of gymnastics, is more suitable than the boys' verse.

We were teased and 'stuffed' with stories of rabbits and hares etc. Big girls in our dormitory of 16 beds told us that on the last day of the month we all had to go to the school gym (across a wide games field) in order to eat chocolate rabbits! Also, on the last day of term, we were due to eat 'Resurrection pudding', which was all the left over puddings every day of the whole term. Children fresh from home believed these fabricated stories implicitly, and during the first week of term had to sing a song to everyone in the dormitory – a terrifying experience for some. A good friend of mine, sadly no longer with us, Madge Farrant, sang the following musical contribution, remembered with laughter for well over 60 years:

> I like scented soap
> As in my bath I frolic.
> But if you give me scented soap
> Don't give carbolic

The following years were more riotous as we sang, 'Star of Wonder, Star of Night', as we travelled through the tunnels on the train up to London.

Miss King was my first form mistress, tall and elegant, and it was her first job. For some unknown reason she appointed me form captain in the second term. What characters our form mistresses were as we travelled upwards through the school. Miss Farrell taught Latin, followed by Miss Constance Smith, later to be met with the Oxford Group of friends; 'Johnny' Walker with bandy legs who bellowed, "Stop that trumpeting" if we dared to prolong nose blowing during a geography lesson; Maggie Mew was Miss Muriel, whose history lessons were a joy, and the footnotes in the text books always so much more interesting than the facts above.

Miss Barrett taught art, and her sister continued later teaching in her place. Pottery was in the new Art School, with a glass cabinet containing a precious piece of 'Ur of the Chaldees' on the wall as we struggled with a coiled pottery (a leaking first effort pot is still around at home).

There was a craze for autograph albums – you handed yours round and everyone contributed a painting or a poem. Lazy ones got the last page, "By hook or by crook I'll be the last in the book."

Top: Miss King and Miss Walker
Bottom left: Miss Barrett and Miss Whittington
Bottom right: Betty Handover (on whom I had a crush)

A regular feature at the end of term was a 'sticking and licking' day where we were supposed to mend with paste and transparent paper our well-worn textbooks. Blankets all had to be taken out and shaken with a friend on the cricket field – was it 12 times each? Friday nights we stood in a line by the sinks to have a spoonful of cascara. At the beginning of term it was daily combing of hair to ensure that we had not brought nits from home. This procedure went on for several weeks.

Health was important, and I remember seeing dumb bells in the gym which were no longer used. Chicken pox could be fun when some of us were sent to recuperate in the large sanatorium (as the infirmary was full of sick children), where we stuck transfers on the wall and slid down the stairs on tin trays. The history of Christ's Hospital is so well documented that I advise any reader interested to visit the school museum at Horsham.

Thursday evenings were mending nights. Every pair of black, ribbed, woollen stockings we wore were decorated with running stitches over the toes and heels in darning wool in order to preserve the fabric. Punishment favoured by the ward monitoresses (prefects) was 'two pairs of running stockings' for serious misdemeanours. This meant days of stitching until the hated task was completed and four new stockings were run for new girls to wear.

During official mending sessions, Miss Mossop read *Red Gauntlet* or *The Rosary,* or other slightly sentimental or historical stories, and much giggling occurred behind her armchair in the soppy parts. Miss Mossop also took my measurements so that Mother could make me a party dress (not that we had many parties), but to my mind it was much too long in the skirt! Our Sunday letters were censored, and before submitting my epistle, I changed the measurements to a shorter (and to my mind, more fashionable) skirt. Of course I was caught out and summoned to Miss Mossop's room. I can remember my tears dripping onto her polished table as she admonished me for dishonesty. I don't remember wearing the blue frilly dress except for a photo with my mother who wore a beautiful evening dress.

Joan Westlake, Elizabeth, Evelyn Woodhouse and another in the production of *Emma* for speech day.

About that time we were treated to a poetry reading afternoon by a famous modern poet, and I never forgot his spring verses about flowers: "Primroyses, Primroyses and Primroyses… and all the little pigs were black." How we laughed at his Welsh vowels, and for years we would repeat the words, but I am sorry that I have never found his poetry since.

Sports Day winners

How we eyed the food left over from dinner on the tables of other wards in the dining hall. Our ward mistress wisely finished up the food allocated to us 35 hungry girls. As we marched out of the dining hall, we gazed longingly at the apple tart or other delicious pudding left uneaten – why were their appetites smaller than ours, we would never know… we could have eaten three helpings.

Potted meat was 'poor father', we thought, so-called after the poem,

> Tell me Mother,
> What is this that looks like strawberry jam?
> Hush Hush my dear
> 'Tis only Pa run over by a tram.

This was on the menu for tea every Friday.

We were always hungry at school. On Sunday nights we crept down the dormitory into the ward kitchen to snaffle pieces of bread left in the baskets. As my best friend's Godmother was the Headmistress, it meant once a term I was invited with her to tea, a terrifying experience. I was given coloured iced cakes, but it was a relief when it was over.

We were bullied, when little, by girls just one form above us. But next year, regretfully, we did the same to new arrivals. It was never done to ask your neighbour to pass the bread; if she didn't like you, you could go hungry for weeks of the term. I well remember starving an upstart of a new girl of pepper for weeks – a specially precious commodity. We later became great friends and corresponded after nearly 50 years – I hope I apologised to her adequately.

What a joy on summer nights to have fire drill. It was too hot to sleep and we stuffed our voluminous calico nightdresses into our 'blues' and clambered into the evening air, down the metal ladders, with terrific excitement.

As regards our official attire, this can be appreciated from the following list of the 1936 Christ's Hospital clothing requirements supplied by the school free of charge:

2 pairs of shoes	1 knickerbockers
2 combinations	1 pinafore
2 pairs drawers	2 pairs stockings
1 tunic	1 coat frock
1 pair of gloves	1 blouse
1 cap	1 coat
2 nightgowns only)	1 velour hat (for best
1 liberty bodice	

Classes were usually a pleasure, except Monday afternoons, when Miss Harding told us to take out our question books in her English Class – terrifying. Mental arithmetic was also misery. Each form was divided into teams, and if all members of a team got all the sums right (ten out of ten), we won a chocolate whipped cream walnut each – a real thrill. How awful you felt if you were the only one to get 9/10, with the rest of the team getting full marks.

No one in my form will ever forget Pat Dick sitting in the front row of desks as she solemnly put her pen in her ink well and threw it at the back of Miss Barton, our dictation mistress, who wore a beautiful new fawn crêpe de chine dress. There was no *Quink* or *Biros* which are easily removed. A disorder mark, or worse, was Pat's fate, and she was doomed to spend every Wednesday afternoon until the end of term cooped up writing lines in the classroom.

Music lessons came and went with terrible regularity. In order to revise before a harmony examination, I used a pencil and quantities of lavatory paper, because with a severe attack of Quinsey, I was not allowed any books. The 'loo bumf' paid dividends as I got 100% and a gold medal. Exams were always looming ahead, and if I fielded 'deep' for cricket matches I could revise with a Latin vocabulary in my pocket if the bowling was slow.

Another friend who benefited from nursing care in the infirmary was Nancy Walland, who had chicken pox and had scratched a spot. As a result she nearly died. I well remember her being delirious and walking in her nightgown down our passage. All the school was asked at evening prayers to sing 'Fight the Good Fight', opening the windows so that our voices reached the sanatorium. She recovered.

During a hot summer's day, Ginger Goodwin and Jocelyn McLean decided (aged 10 or 11) to clamber round the metal beams supporting the upper dormitory. For some reason, known best to themselves, they wore their birthday suits. Unfortunately they were caught when, with a gasp of horror, our ward mistress did a round of inspection unexpectedly.

Each day we had cleaning duties and responsibility for laying the tables for meals etc. One particular senior girl fiercely controlled us as we cleaned the eight basins, with brass taps and plugs etc, in the downstairs cloakroom. Life was rough if you were sloppy with the *Brasso*.

Every night we had ward prayers led by the senior monitoress. Some of us were little snobs, and when one person took prayers, we waited with bated breath for " 'igh," " 'earted," and " 'appiness" in the well known stirring prayer.

I was not brilliant at games, making only the 2nd XI at hockey and the junior rounders team. I had a crush on one of the school tennis team, and hoped she noticed a very good catch I made when playing an away match at Welwyn near the *Shredded Wheat* factory.

Every year I seemed to collect a prize for Scripture work, and also a prize on Sports Day competitions such as the obstacle race, the sack race, or throwing the cricket ball. Music exams were passed regularly until I was awarded the only gold medal for music (Grade VIII) ever produced in the reign of Edward VIII.

Daily attendance at chapel with the Head Mistress laid a foundation for my life. I didn't realise for many years that she was unable to use her left hand, which she kept unnoticed at her side. For many years also she wrote lengthy encouraging letters to me after I had left CH – some of which I still keep. How we feared to behave badly in chapel. Later at school I had to read a daily psalm, or play the hymns on the organ. Being in the choir gave me endless joy. Sadly the chapel was replaced by *Tesco's* when Hertford School was relocated to Horsham.

Confirmation meant a great deal to me. The Bishop of St Albans (Bishop Furze) was full of witty stories. My mother's great friend was the sister of Mervyn Haigh, the Bishop of Coventry, later the famous Bishop of Winchester. "Tell Winifred to take notes," said the Bishop to his sister. To my shame my mother sat writing notes of Furze's sermon during the service because Haigh had eight more confirmations including four public schools, and "not an idea in his head."

When I was in the fourth form (relatively junior) our Ward Monitoress, Madge Farrant, later a distinguished school governor and brilliant teacher of maths at Portsmouth, suggested that I trained the ward for the annual singing competition, sight-reading a psalm and a part song. I taught them *Nymphs and Shepherds* and to our delight we won and continued to win each year until I left school, gaining the singing picture to hang every year in the ward day room.

One job we had in the fifth form was to be in charge of the lower dormitory at night. That meant stopping 16 lively youngsters talking at 8.15 pm – not easy on a bright summer's night. One particular girl taught me a lesson when she drew a picture of me in a blue robe with a large red petticoat beneath, inferring I was a hypocrite myself – something I needed to learn.

Not being bright enough to go in to the sixth form, having only got nine credits in the School Certificate/Matriculation including Distinction in French, I was put in the Housecraft Form (parallel to the sixth form) to do Domestic Science. We put our hair up in buns, no longer pigtails, and we had an immense amount of fun here, especially since the exams I had dreaded since I was nine were over. We also had some very amusing people in our form, and a fascinating form mistress who spent time in cookery lessons telling us about her golf progress, finally climbing onto the table to demonstrate her dancing steps in the forthcoming staff play of *Wind in the Willows* (she was Toad). We laughed immoderately and continued to do so at Old Girls' Day for the next 60 years.

Basically my years at school were full of fear. "You have been given a good education – you must be a credit to your school," so I dared not fool about.

Whilst at Christ's Hospital, all students had to learn and sing the Carmen, the Latin school song (see appendix).

The Charge

I charge you never to forget
the great benefits that
you have received in this place,
and in time come
according to your means
to do all that you can
to enable others to enjoy the
same advantage;
and remember that you carry
with you, wherever you go,
the good name
of Christ's Hospital.
May God Almighty
bless you in your ways and
keep in you the
knowledge of his love
now and forever.

When we left school aged 17½ we had to wear our own clothes home on the train, and the stress of what to wear occupied many hours of our thinking – one had to wear mufti in front of school friends who had never seen us (except if they had visited us at home) wearing anything but school uniform.

Above all we need young men and women who by godly discipline and purpose in their own lives can give our youth a new direction

Hope for Today, Grosvenor Books

Dance Until You Drop

I had always loved dancing, and this became even more of a passion when I had lessons for Greek Dancing at the age of 17. Maybe my first pantomime gave me the urge to go on the stage; the Evershed family had invited me, aged five, to join their children for a pantomime in Birmingham. It was a great thrill, where real water was splashed over theatrical rocks in one scene, and later cuddly toys were thrown to the audience – needless to say those of us in a box got a generous share.

My headmistress must have felt that I had some talent for dance because she suggested that I considered going on to a dance and drama school. I was excited by this prospect, considerably more so than my mother, but gradually she was won over. I was fortunate in gaining the necessary funding from the Girls' Realm Guild, and so it was that I went to Ginner Mawer School of Dance and Drama in Earls Court.

For the first year I lived with my grandmother in Sidcup. Drama was based at Philbeach Gardens, where we worked from 9.30 am – 5.30 pm, and when performing in the evenings at the Albert Hall, it meant tearing down long passages of the South Kensington Underground Station to catch the last train back to Sidcup. Early on in our training we had to perform in *Elijah* – why we were dancing as priests I do not remember. At the stirring chorus, 'Baal we cry to thee', followed by an explosion of fire later in Handel's Oratorio, something went very wrong. We stood imploring the heavens and instead of an almighty flash a small balloon wandered up towards the roof of the Albert Hall. The music carried on.

During the summer we performed dances in Hyde Park and sometimes ventured to perform in areas such as Surbiton. One very cold windy day we were filmed as Greek maidens and goddesses near Aldershot on a golf course, together with self-conscious London policeman as Greek gentleman in exceedingly short, unbecoming outfits. There was much laughter, but we got lovely packed lunches, as I think it was for an advertisement.

The life of Prince Siddhartha, the son of the Buddha, caused us to become Nautch girls at a large London theatre. "Eyes and teeth, girls," Miss Ginner used to shout at us, encouraging us to look seductive.

Prince Siddhartha

70

Weekends were often occupied. On one occasion I was the back legs of an elephant at the Aldwych Theatre, and *Noah's Ark* was forever in our repertoire. We were involved in shows such as marching at Wembley Stadium in front of Princess Elizabeth with other groups including the Women's Institute and Women's League of Health and Beauty. We also performed with other representatives from all over Britain, participating in our now familiar Albert Hall.

This venue was our home in February. It was freezing cold as we lay as chorus girls on the rough mats, Markova in fur coat and high heels walking her part. Other performances included being the crowd in a sacred pageant, *The King of Glory,* again in skimpy cheap costumes – not helpful if one's entrance was right and your dressing room left... just try running round the corridors if you are late for your entrance!

Greek dancing on a Surrey golf course

The theory of dancing, history of mime, Greek Mythology, and all the other 13 subjects that we had in our annual exams, were not such a strain as the physical effort needed. Not having danced until aged 17, I was competing with other students who, at expensive schools such as Roedean, Royal School Bath, and Westonbirt, had danced since very early childhood. No wonder I was stuck at the back of Greek tragedies as a column or a tree!

To begin ballet dancing at so late an age, having never done anything but a little holiday Greek dancing in the garden, was hell, and my toes were bleeding from ballet shoes when we came off the stage. However, Peggy van Praag, a famous dancer at Covent Garden, coached me on a Sunday in her own flat, her cousin Madge having got me through the teacher's exam. I was the only one in my set to pass, and they had all learnt ballet at school. Greek dancing was hard, as was national dancing, when we galloped around in red Russian boots when necessary.

My undoing the first term was having to design the dance I was going to teach. Miss Ginner ran the dancing school with Miss Mawer and I visualised our skipping round the room, tripping lightly over a plan of a huge 'G' and a very thin 'M'. It was not until this suggestion met with a cold reception from Miss Ginner that I realised she was an extremely fat lady, and her colleague Miss Mawer extremely thin.

When I tried to do long leaps I tended to knock into smaller girls and incur much wrath thereby. When we danced with Markova at the Albert Hall, the photographs excluded me and concentrated on those whom we named the 'Beauts'. How thrilled I was finally to see a photograph of Markova in the popular *Sketch* (rather like the *Hello* of the day) with Cleone Chadwick and me behind. I have swanked about this ever since!

How I got through my finals I do not know, and the sister of *The Daily Telegraph* critic, Miss Agate, said that my performance of *Prometheus Bound* (translated by Gilbert Murray) was the nearest to Sarah Bernhard she had ever seen. To me it personified what Christ went through on the cross, and I did my best to portray that conception. My mother sat in the audience at the end of the play with a friend.

In my second year I took digs in Earls Court, and on Sundays the tinkle of the muffin man's bell drew me out to the little balcony. I had bed, breakfast and Sunday meals for £2/2 a week, and so I was always hungry, especially as I was dancing all the time. How I longed to afford the hot delicious-smelling muffins, but my grant did not stretch to such luxuries. I often paid 4½p for my lunch – a small brown loaf lasted a week with a pot of paste, and possibly an orange and an egg prepared in my digs in Trebovir Road.

Photograph from *The Sketch*

Elizabeth the Dancer

Markova

The hunger and cold persisted throughout my training. I 'fain would have been filled' with the awful 'colour scheme' of unsweetened black currant pudding that we were given at Christ's Hospital. When there, a visiting Governor had seen a hungry child with 'pass-ons' on her plate from both neighbours – we were then prescribed custard.

Pageant that I produced at Bowood
On the right is Lady Elizabeth Lansdowne wearing a black shawl
The little children are dressed as deer

Meanwhile my dancing training continued. Holidays meant more courses, more study, and more disciplined ballet exercises in the bathroom – one dare not slacken. One summer I stayed with my aunt near Hampton Court and had to look after my cousin Colin after an absolutely exhausting day dancing in London. Colin had locked himself into a cupboard, refusing to go to bed. Later he became a brilliant architect, and his brother had a senior position in the army in the Middle East. Our principal, Miss Ginner, said, "You go on until you drop dead, and then get up and go on dancing."

Their younger sister, Heather, was a nurse in 'Barts', and we all loved her wedding in the famous hospital chapel. Their (great?) grandfather, Edwin Sydney Woodiwiss, built the North Staffordshire railway, and had an enormous house with wonderful cedar trees. Great Uncle Sydney was known as a breeder of Dachshunds dogs. One day a performer who made poems of surnames appeared in the town. He was given Woodiwiss as a task by my Great Aunt Cossie. Quick as lightning came the retort, "If I had a Dachshund, would I whisper in his ear?"

When staying near the Palace of Hampton Court, I didn't remember that my great aunt, the General's wife, had lived in a tiny grace and favour flat there. On one occasion, King Edward and Queen Alexander visited her and tactfully said (seeing the size of her kitchen), "Oh, Mrs Udney, how delightfully hot your gravies must be." One imagined the journey from Buckingham Palace kitchens to the dining room must have cooled the King's gravy.

Soon afterwards I had a black-out in a mime theory exam and had to leave the room – it was an empty page, and I realise now that it must have been the onset of my illness. I had worked until three o'clock the night before. None of my aunts in the house realised the stress. Likewise, my room-mate, when I later had a breakdown, was completely unaware that I was ill.

Hill Place, Upminster, amidst acres of cedar trees,
home of Auntie Cossie & Uncle Sydney Woodiwiss

Aunt Cossie

Turning out papers recently, I discovered the programme of our final students' production, and was amazed at the variety and ability shown at the Rudolph Steiner Hall (near Baker Street). The previous year, Cleone Chadwick and Rachel Sinclair Thompson had been sails in my rocking, sailing boat dance, as I chanted "Back and forward" (to the well known Schumann music). It became known as the 'BF dance' with much laughter.

In the last year of our training, the play "what I wrote" (to quote Morecambe and Wise) was a medieval mime, the *Woe of the Needy* from Piers Plowman. Each one of us finalists were in a vast variety of items – I know rehearsing was a nightmare, but it was 'all right on the night'.

A holiday after three devastating years of work meant my mother's great friend, Marguerite Stocker, going with us for a holiday in Llandudno. Marguerite was incredibly generous to my aunts and mother when she died. We went to a 'posh' hotel, and as war was about to break out I took my stockings into the lounge to mend (having carefully mended clothes for years). I was severely told off, and the mending and I were banished to my bedroom. In the hotel we listened to Chamberlain pronounce, "Britain is at war."

In that February we had all begun to apply for teaching jobs, to begin in September 1939. Little did we think that war would break out a few days before we began work.

To my amazement I got the coveted job as Dance and Drama teacher at Westonbirt, but then the venue changed, placing the children at Corsham Court and Bowood near Chippenham, the homes of Lord Methuen and Lord Lansdowne respectively. Spye Court was also used, and staff were billeted with the local families. The brilliant art mistress Bridget Peterson and I slept in a room full of wonderful furniture, and Miss Posniakov had another equally beautiful bedroom nearby. We shared a bathroom, and each day a maid woke us with a copper can of blazing hot water for washing and clean linen towels. Unfortunately in my enthusiasm to get to the bathroom, I fell and broke some of the priceless banisters on the stairs – I was not a popular guest!

On Sundays, after taking the children to the nearby church at Derry Hill, we had lunch with Lord and Lady Walter Hervey – our host and hostess. We used our finger bowls and tried to remember what the sermon was about. At teatime we emerged from our rooms to the drawing room where Lady Hervey presided over the tea table with silver kettle boiling and hot muffins. Some days I was allowed to play their lovely grand piano, when everyone had left the room.

Westonbirt was a challenge because the girls I taught had so much money, which we never had at Christ's Hospital, and I did not understand their needs because they had all the material things of which I had been deprived.

We had no netball pitches marked out, so I had to work in a cow field without any knowledge of measurements or how to work a marker. In the job description I was meant to teach golf and lacrosse, so between February and September I worked madly to learn both games – racing round our field at Bosham, learning to cradle the lacrosse stick, and then attempting to learn the rudiments of golf. At Bowood there were no fields suitable for lacrosse, and to my relief no golf course. As there were no facilities for either game; I just taught dancing, drama, remedial exercises and games. Later, when practising chipping with Mr Denis Thatcher at Lamberhurst Golf Course, I asked him to give the winning nurses a shield in the auxiliary nursing competition we organised, so perhaps those 1939 lessons bore some fruit.

One memorable day the Queen decided to pay us a visit – a very frightening experience. "Gloomy," she said, as she entered the staff room where we were digging into wartime scones. The top windows were covered with black-out papers all day. We all bobbed curtseys, having waited so long for her to arrive, clutching our tea cups. She proceeded to the dormitories. The Matron, having only been alerted recently, had shoved the laundry higgledy-piggledy into drawers – as usual Her Majesty just had to look into them. In the dining room she saw the children. "Very nice – brown bread and honey," she said. "Oh, there's a wasp," and she seized a knife and began swatting. "Allow me," said the Earl of Athlone, and finished off the insect.

As a junior dancing mistress, my duty was to teach the whole school to curtsey, following which the gym mistress taught them all something quite different. After tea I went to take prep in the library, where all the walls were lined with priceless Gainsborough paintings. Of course, Her Majesty had to come in. Lady Lansdowne said, "This is Miss Coxon, she teaches Elizabeth (her daughter) dancing." "What are you doing?" asked the Queen. "I'm taking preparation M'am," I said, bobbing the curtsey for all I was worth.

Having personally met Her Majesty, Queen Mary, I remember stories my mother told of her great friend Monica Haigh (sister of Reverend Mervyn Haigh, the Royal Chaplain). When Bognor was chosen for George VI to recuperate, his personal chaplain went to a small cottage nearby with his mother, sister and family nurse. Some years later the family moved to Norham Road, Oxford, and this nurse looked after me when I stayed with them. She was very old then, and I was pleased to learn that, later, she reached her 100th birthday!

As Nurse prepared tea in Bognor, the Queen sent word that she would like to visit the Haigh family, and there was the usual panic of clearing up. Everything was put in the bathroom and the door firmly locked.

The family sat in the small cottage sitting room waiting patiently for the royal Daimler to arrive, when there was a tinkle at the back door. Nurse ignored this first, but when it was repeated she got up with very bad grace and shouted, "You silly milkman; I told you only to leave three pints." The bell sounded again, so stumbling down the backstairs Nurse opened the door. There stood Her Majesty! "I'm sorry, but it is such a lovely sunny day that I decided to walk across the fields," she said as Nurse backed awkwardly upstairs and let the Queen in.

Tea served, the Queen announced that she would like to see the little house, "…and what's in here," she said, rattling the bathroom door, and, of course, truth must out!

The Queen's usual method was to admire any particularly beautiful (or valuable) item in a house, continually returning to have another look. Inevitably, the owner would feel compelled to say, "Your Majesty, please accept it."

The Queen did much to economise when she was first at Buckingham Palace. History has it that when the later Queen Mother, Elizabeth and her husband came unexpectedly to lunch, Queen Mary said, "You, Bertie, will have to sit at the side table and have cold ham and jelly – my guests will have pheasant, but there is only enough for us."

Her Majesty used to attend Holy Communion in the early morning. One day a member of the congregation, who was wearing a scarf, came up to him and said, "That was very nice, Mr Haigh. The deep voice sounded familiar to the chaplain, and when the lady had left the royal chapel he realised it was Queen Mary without her wig!

During the war, when Coventry was suffering from the appalling bombing, Queen Elizabeth asked to visit the city, and after witnessing the devastation for herself and spending time with the people of the city, she lunched with Mervyn Haigh, who was now the bishop. As he apologised for the non-matching crockery on which the meal was served, Her Majesty, who had recently been bombed at Buckingham Palace, said, "We have that trouble also." He was later promoted to become Bishop of Winchester.

One day, needing to do shopping in Chippenham, I saw the private train coming from Bowood, so I put my umbrella out, as if stopping a bus. Lord Lansdowne's train kindly drew to a halt and I was able to travel in comfort. The station belonging to his Lordship was known as the Black Dog (no doubt suffering soon afterwards from Dr Beeching).

As was my wont, whilst at Westonbirt, I was attracted by the steward (about the only male in the region) – the same pattern as in my school days which I put down to a lifetime of no males in the family. I always needed an excuse to go down to the village in case I could catch a glimpse of him!

It was in about 1941, whilst working at Westonbirt, that all the pressures on me became too much and I had a breakdown. However, before proceeding with my story I need to take a step back to 1936 and school holidays in Bosham, living with my mother. The crackling telephone allowed us to pass on particularly juicy bits of village gossip to a friend. We added, "That's so, isn't it Sophie?" and the Post Office lady who put us through and was listening avidly said, "Yes." Our small sailing boat, a 12 foot *National*, was shared with Nancy Wilson whose brother Alan was requested to teach me to sail. Neither of us enjoyed the experience, though at the age of 80 plus we still exchange Christmas cards.

Our mothers used to meet regularly for Oxford Group occasions, and we youngsters went for paper chases on the Downs. On one occasion I had to be piggy-backed as one of the 'hares'. Later my Aunt Audrey asked me to go with her to a Billy Graham mission – the counsellor whom she met there remained a life-long friend.

Bosham, and the windows where the aunts escaped

In 1936 our gardens and house in Bosham were the venue for an Oxford Group meeting and from then onwards our home was used to entertain people from all over the world who worked or associated with the Oxford Group (then Moral Rearmament, now Initiatives for Change). This movement began in 1908, using the ideas of Frank Buchman, whereby one lives by the four absolutes – honesty, purity, unselfishness and love, listening daily to the guidance of God, preferably for an hour early in the morning.

My friend Bridget who shared my room at Lord Walter Hervey's home in Calne (Derry Hill) was a wonderful ambassador for the Oxford Group, making friends with the daughters of world leaders such as the famous Burmese politician who was later assassinated. At 6.00 am Bridget had her daily quiet time, and this meant I had to 'share'. The need to confess every sin against the four absolute standards was good discipline.

One day in about 1936 my mother walked back from church feeling the Church of England service did not 'seem to be doing anything'. Her friend, Emily Wilson, said that what had saved her marriage to one of the engineers of the famous Mulberry Harbour was the Oxford Group. Immediately my mother began reading books and finally went to *Brown's Hotel* in London where she was put in touch with Mrs Anson who lived at Farnborough, near my grandmother's house at Sidcup.

To us as a family, my mother's enthusiasm with the Oxford Group was something which helped her immensely spiritually. As an only daughter, I went along with the meetings, house parties, and other organised activities, which became part of my mother's life. However, the strain of my leaving the secure Christian background of Christ's Hospital, and the intense work of training for three years of demanding physical and mental work for dancing and drama, caused my breakdown, and I had to be sent to St Anne's Sanatorium for three months, and so ended my work at Westonbirt.

After three months in hospital, doctors felt that I could do land work, so I helped at a nursery in Sussex belonging to a friend. However, as often as not we were in the ditches, as the 'dog-fights' were above our heads, and we watched anxiously as airmen parachuted towards us – were they theirs or ours?

Later I was allowed to join the Land Army proper, with the famous uniform. I had to drive daily to the cowshed, sit on a three-legged stool to do the milking, then go back to bottle up and drive round Fishbourne delivering. People were so kind in cold weather, giving hot cups of tea, but with no village conveniences I suppose I must have found some bushes!

One Sunday the local doctor, who had a beautiful Jersey cow, asked me to milk it on his gardener's day off, and a wonderful tea was laid on afterwards. To my dismay the cow got out and I was terrified as it neared the barbed wire, but thankfully all was well.

Having knocked a wall down with my milk van, I was not reprimanded by my farmer, as I only had a provisional driving licence. This stood me in good stead until I started driving again (with lessons) as a pupil midwife in the 1960s.

I continued Land Army work, milking by hand at 4.30 am. After milking we were expected to hoe beet, or in the season help with the haymaking. As I write this, I am watching a television programme about the Fishbourne Palace created by the Roman occupation of Britain. We did not imagine as we forked the hay up onto the cart in 1941 that beneath our feet were these magnificent mosaics waiting to be discovered.

> Let gratitude for the past inspire us with trust for the future.
>
> Francois Fenelon 1651-1715.

On days when the inspectors came to look at our cattle I was told to drive some of them into the woods out of sight. I did not know that they had TB – ah well, there was a war on.

After putting the cardboard tops on the bottles, the rats decided they wanted a drink at night. "What shall I do?" I asked the farmer. "Put some fresh cardboard disks on the bottles," said he. Ah well, what the eye doesn't see… I hadn't trained as a nurse at this time and dared not complain.

When I fell and got a badly infected leg, I asked for time off. "Don't you know that there's a war on – we haven't time for a breakdown," said Lady Reading, the boss of the Land Army in Britain. After my leg injury I was unable to return home, so I had to stay at Funtingdon Down with friends of my mother. She had been so shocked by my illness she let our house in Bosham and helped cook in the home of some Moral Rearmament friends.

Whilst I was recuperating from my breakdown I discovered that I could apply for a job on the stage because it was a reserved occupation. So, with great trepidation I appeared at Drury Lane stage door. My dear Aunt Edythe Taylor, wife of the Mayor of Wembley, had me to stay. "Next," shouted the producer, so I gave the accompanist 'The Gentle Maiden' and 'I'll Walk Beside You', and having sung my heart out proceeded to perform my best Irish jig technique. "Thank ya, we'll be in touch," convinced me that ENSA did not want my talents.

One of the girls said, "If you go round the corner they are rehearsing for *Rosemarie*, Tom Arnold's number two company. I did and was successful, so now started nine months touring Britain for £5 a week in 1942. Often we did not know where we would sleep until we arrived – Cardiff, Halifax, Brighton, Oldham, Golder's Green etc, a different town each week. We performed six evening shows and two matinees, and in each session we had 12 changes of costume. If we were near enough to friends or family we could be sure of a decent meal and a bath, otherwise it was pot luck.

Attached to most theatres was a chaplain from the Actors' Church Union, to which I belonged. A delightful vicar, Reverend Hardie, met me at the stage door one day and asked me to stay with his family. The cast of *Rosemarie* nominated me the 'vicar's plaything'.

Not long afterwards I was asked to be Godmother to their daughter, Janice, who later married a doctor and they have a talented family.

I thoroughly enjoyed my time touring, but I felt this life was not helping us win the war, so I applied to be a nurse.

The care I had received as I recovered from my breakdown inspired me to become a nurse. The Harley Street consultant told my mother that I must never have a senior responsible job! I was determined to prove him wrong.

Initiatives of Change

This chapter reviews my time with the Oxford Group/MRA before proceeding further into my story.

On my first day of nursing in 1942 I waltzed into the Kentish Hospital sluice with a bedpan to meet, unexpectedly, Kathleen Ledger, a keen Oxford Group personality with whom I was later to work for many years in the MRA activities. During the war, positive leaflets were distributed to help maintain morale. Plays were written and acted, and the beautiful estate of Tirley Garth in Cheshire, given by Miss Irene Prestwich, was used as a home for service men and women. Here meetings were held and folk from the army, navy, and air force met during their leave. They continued to have meetings and share their spiritual battles whilst taking part in running the house and garden in the lovely countryside, away from active war service.

I find this a very difficult chapter, as this movement, the Oxford Group, has been a tremendous influence in my life giving me much but causing me – if I am absolutely honest – many years of pain. The other three absolutes, purity, unselfishness and love, were the guiding points in the teaching we received, and the way of life we tried to follow, albeit often very unsuccessfully.

When I married, my husband had a very unbiased approach to my male friends whom I had 'put on pedestals', and for the first time I realised Ted had an interesting point of view.

For years I had gone along with my mother's enthusiastic opinions that MRA people were right and my ideas, which did not agree, were wrong. I had felt God wanted me to fit in and 'not rock the boat', but now I was faced with a much-loved husband who, as an experienced man of the world, felt my friends had faults.

All my life previously my mother had made her house available to me, but I must admit I 'conformed' as I was getting free board and lodging (though paying my expenses), and hoped to inherit the house on my mother's death. This meant agreeing to carry out duties and responsibilities, helping with the MRA work that in later life some of which I abandoned after my mother's death. The attitude and humility of MRA folk changed in the 1990s and I work happily with I/C folk now.

> Grant to us O Lord the royalty of inward happiness and the serenity, which comes from living close to Thee. Daily renew in us the sense of joy, filling every corner of our hearts with light and grace; so that bearing about with us the infection of a good courage, we may be diffusers of life and may meet all ills and cross accidents with gallant and high-hearted happiness, giving Thee thanks for all things.
>
> Robert Louis Stevenson 1850-94

My mother was extremely hospitable and welcomed anyone from the village with alacrity. However, her sisters, enjoying a peaceful holiday at Bosham sitting by the fire, were not so charitable. On one occasion the front door bell took her to see the visitors. "Do come in and meet my sisters," she said. Meanwhile my two aunts quickly opened the drawing room window and made a hasty exit, lying on the ground so as not to be seen. As the visitors entered, no sign of an aunt was visible, to my mother's extreme embarrassment.

Nancy, the elder sister, was anxious to help with our production of *A Christmas Carol*. Unfortunately the 1930s *Hoover* was very loud, and her sound effects of the ghosts' appearance on stage completely drowned the text being declared by my cousins.

A wartime saving my mother made was to encourage us all to cut up dozens of apples into rings, which she hung round the kitchen to dry and rehydrate at a later occasion. She had, however, forgotten that to keep our old fashioned fire acting efficiently we had to riddle the ashes daily, with the result that the apples were progressively covered with soot and ash as the days went by, until finally they were quite inedible. Our evacuees from London were not 'house trained' and bed linen had to be changed frequently. Finally, they could not bear the quietness of the village, and missing *Woolworth's* and fish and chips, took the whole family back to London.

My cousin Daphne's memory is far better than mine and she recalls details brilliantly. I do remember, however, when on a freezing day after Aunt Nancy had hung the washing on the line in the vicarage garden Daphne, aged seven, came in announcing that the sheets were board stiff!

One Christmas my mother, fired with enthusiasm, invited a whole gypsy family to dinner. All arrived with much enthusiasm, except Percy. The 13-year-old insisted on staying by the gate for the whole of Christmas afternoon in the cold. When asked where he was, his mother said, "Percy's stooborn." Later my mother got him a job in a London hotel as 'Buttons' – stubbornness had paid off.

When her energies were channelled into supporting the Oxford Group from the 1930s onwards, our house was filled with visitors from all over the world. During the war many helpers at the headquarters in Berkeley Square in London would live in our home. They would all go daily to do secretarial or domestic work supporting the growing numbers of people attending meetings, or provide hospitality for distinguished guests in government and influential circles. I remember waiting on Kagawa after the war, an eminent Japanese Christian philosopher.

"Do you know anyone who speaks French and can work as a housekeeper at the Consulate of Laos?" This question was put to my good friends Dr Ken and Mrs Frances McAll in 1955. I had enjoyed my time living with them; however, after nearly two years living on faith and prayer, I was ready to move on into the fairly empty home of MRA friends at Wilton Crescent London.

Staff was provided by the Chargé d'Affairs, Monsieur Sauvanovang. This included a Chinese Nanny for the six children who had all been in Paris consuming sweets galore. After Asian food this was disastrous, so one of my first duties was to take them to an MRA dentist in Harley Street for umpteen fillings for their teeth. Domestic help was provided by Hilde, a German parlour maid; there was an English butler, and dailies whom I appointed (with complete ignorance on my part). The first important job was to find a flagpole for the Laotian flag, which I finally discovered in *Gamages*, and enjoyed putting it on our balcony.

Ambassadors' wives then began arriving, and fortunately another friend, Barbara Chidell, came to my aid – she had taught the King and Queen of Siam (Thailand), and having recently been to her wedding (when she was 60) I felt I could ask her to come and meet the ambassadors' wives for coffee and tea. Fortunately the butler knew enough of the court procedure to encourage the Ambassador to change his trousers (pin stripe to black) before travelling in the official carriage to Buckingham Palace.

On one occasion, the Princess from Laos unexpectedly came for lunch. I had cooked a light meal for the staff – my pastry being of very poor quality. "Don't worry," said the Ambassador, "just give her melon." Someone tore round Knightsbridge collecting *Harrod's* best fruit, and all was well until the Princess asked, "Is there anything else?" "There is some jam tart which Miss Coxon made for the staff," said the Butler. "I will have some jam stark," said

Her Highness, and up came my tired cooking effort. It was pretty hard and shot across the table!

One evening I got a call at 1.00 am from the Ambassador. Tucked up in bed, I hurriedly dressed, remade the fire and found drinks as the French Ambassador had decided to call.

Much as I loved the Laotian family, who invited me back with them to teach the family English, I was advised that my phone calls were being bugged and that it was not safe. This was 1955. The devastating war soon after made me realise that God had prevented me from going back to their country with them. However, before I get too ahead of my story, I shall now return to 1942/3 when I started my nursing career.

Chorus Girl with Bedpans

With firmness in the right as God gives us to see the right, let us strive to finish the work we are in.

Abraham Lincoln.

As mentioned earlier, after nine months as a back row Chorus Girl, I went to stay with my Grandmother in Sidcup, having felt the need to do something more useful in the war. Applying to nurse in Kent found me behind a desk facing Mavis Hastie, a friend from Christ's Hospital, who has since become a Nun in Edgware. She sent me for two weeks of training at Willesborough, an old Cottage Hospital, where we slept 16 in a dormitory and learned how to give out bedpans. After a week a telegram arrived, telling me to report at 9.00 am on Monday to Kent and Canterbury Hospital.

On the Monday morning we met in Matron's Office in awkward Nursing Auxiliaries' uniform, our caps flying off with the greatest of ease, and we were made welcome by the famous Miss Purchas MBE. Matron was tall, with very long legs which seemed to twist round each other as she sat at her office desk and we confessed to breaking yet another glass thermometer. Somehow, when she did the daily ward round, the large safety pin holding my apron often seemed to come adrift with disastrous results.

We earned one pound a week, and had to buy stockings and other necessities, but were fed and housed free of charge. Having been a patient in hospital for so many months, the thought of exams and another career were terrifying, even though one subject was cookery. Our first billet in Norman Road provided no hot water or food and we ate in the hospital. As hot water bottles were unavailable, we filled glass lemonade bottles in hospital a mile away. On duty at 7.00 am after an inadequate slither of Spam and bread, hot cups of tea were welcome. We gathered in Sister's office for the Night Nurse's report. "Put your hair behind your ears, Nurse," Sister shouted at me on my first morning. The cherished pageboy style of the chorus girl became an unsightly bun for the next 20 years. Staff Nurse bullied us into making the 50 or so beds before Sister came on duty.

We struggled to care for chaps from D-Day, as they had poured in before being evacuated to hospitals in the North of England. Later, alone on night duty, one turned to the Almighty for His support.

Sisters, with their crackling aprons and neat caps, ruled our lives on and off duty, even in the Nurses' Home. Housemen were always tired, and consultants were gods. Each evening we staggered with enormous black-out screens as the newly-built pre-war hospital had acres of glassed-in balconies. Folding dirty wet sheets at midnight, ready for the laundry, while German bombers flew over us, was not a happy experience.

On Sunday evenings the Hospital Chaplain took Evensong on the wards, and two of us carried the portable organ from ward to ward for Matron to play the hymns. Christmas dances were a bit of a strain as she and senior members of staff sat at the end of the nurses' sitting room, whilst invited guests from local Army barracks, Air Force stations and Navy headquarters steered us round sedately. The 10.00 pm curfew was slightly extended that night, but we enjoyed ourselves when invited back to our guests' workplaces (Army headquarters, RAF stations, etc) on other occasions.

During the war we were always hungry. On VE-Day an un-iced cake that had gone mouldy arrived in the post. Coming off duty, I ran a full bath (after four years of only five inches) and sat luxuriating, demolishing the whole cake which my dear Mother had sent, mildew and all.

During the war we visited Canterbury Cathedral in our off-duty periods, a privilege and an inspiration. Many of the priceless stained glass windows had been removed for fear of bombs. We could watch the famous 'Red Dean', so called for his left-wing tendencies, combing his hair as he left the vestry. His daughters both had their tonsils and their adenoids removed in our private wards. Aunt Nancy had moved to Mark Cross near Tunbridge Wells, and Daphne used to take me to Burrswood, the Home of Healing founded by Dorothy Kerrins, at Groombridge. Years afterwards I remember seeing Bunny Austin, the famous tennis player, there as a patient.

Canterbury Cathedral Service at the end of the war

Daphne was a favourite of Dean Inge when she was a child, as he had lost his three-year-old daughter. Other visitors to the How's home in Shrewsbury included Bishop Walsham How who wrote *For All the Saints*. As Mr How was Uncle Tudor's church warden, breakfast was a duty for my godmother, Aunt Nancy. A light remark such as, "Do you think it will rain today?" was relayed and repeated all the length of the huge table for the edification of the distinctly deaf Dean, and the extreme embarrassment of my godmother over their bacon and eggs.

Nancy (my godmother) and Tudor Owen, parents of John and Daphne

Before I digress any further, I must mention my cousin John, Daphne's brother, who, as a six-year-old, was filled with umpteen slices of bread and butter before being taken to children's parties, so as not to disgrace the vicarage. Having nevertheless demolished the chocolate biscuits, he was very sick on returning home, but announced to the family, "It couldn't have been the chocolate biscuits as I only had 15 and the other boy had 20." Little was I to realise the dangers he would later endure in the Far East as a Major in the Army, whilst I pranced round with bedpans when men returned from D-Day before being transferred to hospitals in the north of England.

On holiday I worked on the land in Norwich and Peterborough, and later got to Lincoln and Ely Cathedrals, which were all beautiful and uplifting experiences. Litchfield provided a wonderful performance of Dorothy Sayers' *A Man Born to be King*, a most moving play that I have never forgotten. Mystery plays, written in medieval times, were also a delight, with brilliant acting, and they included devils, realistic animals, and angels descending from the towering vaulted cathedral roofs.

Moving around in the war, I caught sight of Clark Gable in US Army uniform on Peterborough Station. He was a little man, so different from his imposing film appearance, who inspired us as youngsters to take part in 'King Arthur's Tales', with my cousins as 'Knights of the Green Table'; peering over the vicarage clothes horse covered by a blanket, pretending to lean over the eastern castle walls!

Our main relaxation as nurses was to put on plays and entertainments. Christmas pantomimes were notorious for consultants dressing up as nurses, and sisters sometimes also took part. One year Home Sister Evans, known as Bertha, produced our Nativity play. In order to economise on toilet paper we used tow for bedpan purposes – long pieces of shredded sacking. This provided Sister with a very satisfactory wig which she wore as long blonde plaits – I cannot remember how this fitted into the Christmas story, but it did! Years later she married a priest attached to the Cathedral, and she was one Sister whom we loved.

Our Pageant of Nursing needed my appearance as the 'Spirit of Nursing' at the beginning of each scene, grasping a lamp and dolled out in a long blue Grecian outfit found in someone's dressing up box. Having taught my friends Egyptian arm movements (remembered from my dance training) in scene two, hefty third year nurses cavorted to the accompaniment of a Grieg's Holberg suite on a wind-up gramophone. It seemed to amuse the nursing and medical staff when Canterbury was being blitzed.

Gypsies used to manage to have their babies during the hop picking and fruit gathering periods. One nice person named Mrs Smith, naturally, had long plaits of unusually fair hair and kept her bed immaculately tidy, obviously having lived all her life in the confined space of a caravan. Many years later, on one evening in about 1968, I drove up Colt's Hill near Pembury, a notorious accident spot now, and saw a hop picker walking. Without a second thought, after having so many of his family and friends in my wards, I offered him a lift to the village in my little *Morris*, which he accepted with alacrity. When I returned home my mother was none too pleased. Such was our confidence in relatives of our patients we had none of the fear nurses have today. When an old gypsy was dying on the medical ward, 70 relatives gathered in the waiting room. I understand the ward sister used all her air freshener after they left. Soon afterwards I passed the scorched green where, true to tradition, the caravan of the deceased was burnt in its entirety.

Pupil Midwives working in the East End of London likewise were safe (we had to wear little bonnets and cloaks travelling to those notorious Peabody Buildings with very steep staircases). The problem, however, in East Ham Town Hall, during the Maternity Hospital's annual sale of work, was that we only had to turn our backs on our stall to discover a proportion of our precious goods disappeared into capacious shopping bags.

How we managed to pass our SRN exams, as well as our hospital finals, I shall never know. "Be careful with that injection, Nurse, it costs £5 per bottle (five weeks' salary)." Streptomycin was the newest drug we used on Nuffield One Ward at the Radcliffe Hospital in Oxford where I moved when I qualified. Our Consultant in the Neurosurgical Department was Professor Cairns, who had recently been sent for when Lawrence of Arabia had his fatal motorbike accident, but it was too late. Nearly all our patients were unconscious. I remember the professor opening a man's skull like a tin of baked beans and performing a miraculous operation – and the man survived.

Off duty we were in the midst of post-war jubilation. There were university May week balls at Merton and Keble, dancing until dawn, then in a punt for breakfast. When working in the hospital one day, a good friend told me I looked like the advertisement, 'Keep death off the roads', prevalent at that time, so I bought a five shilling copy of J B Priestley's *An Inspector Calls*, went for an audition at the Oxford Playhouse, and immediately got a part. The hospital released me, as there were plenty of nurses, and next week I was appointed Assistant Stage Manager.

There followed a glorious few months, putting mattresses back stage for actors to fall upon, and filling silver tea pots with boiling water so audiences in the front row could see the steam in a play by Chekhov.

In the autumn a nurse's job awaited me in Australia, and the wooden trunk was ready and labelled. Suddenly my Aunt Olive Prince sent me an advertisement from *The Times* for a dance and drama teacher from my training school to work in Switzerland at Les Avents sur Montreux, the next village to the newly-opened Mountain House at Caux. For many years this was the International Centre for Moral Rearmament. I quickly sent a telegram advising of my change of address, relabelled my trunk to Switzerland and cancelled my job in Sydney.

Chatelard School Les Avants (modern picture)

The new job involved teaching dancing, skiing, skating and speaking French at meals. Weekend duties included taking the little ones shopping and teaching music. Frozen flooded tennis courts, when flood-lit, enabled the children to skate, clutching buns and mugs of cocoa. At last there was enough to eat. The parents of one pupil, living in England at the *Ritz Hotel*, asked their daughter to bring home food for them at the end of term. Those of us who had lived in Doodle-bug alley, watching those horrible machines as we tried to concentrate on anatomy lessons, enjoyed the wonderful croissants and creamy coffee each morning as we looked out to the French mountains overlooking Lake Geneva.

After a year in Switzerland I returned to work in Sussex, my decision being due in part to learning that Graeme Laird, my heart-throb since childhood, had married another. During my time away, my grandmother had died.

Working at Tortington Park, a Roman Catholic school near Arundel, gave me a lot of experience. Every week one form of girls performed in a play that I had to produce. Children were taken to church on Sunday, and occasionally Queen Elizabeth came too. We had taken the children to Windsor Great Park to see the flowers after her father's death, but queuing for about four hours was not easy as some children were only eight years old.

When we had an epidemic of chickenpox I was asked to work in the infirmary at a reduced salary. The drama work I was doing did not please my boss, and I really enjoyed nursing the children. However, my pride was hurt, and becoming ill I was taken by my mother to visit our friends, Dr Ken McAll with his wife Frances, also a GP. It was therefore a great thrill to get not only medical advice but also an invitation to live in their home in Knyverton Road in Bournemouth.

An exceedingly busy two years followed as Frances and Ken had hundreds of patients, three school age children, and Graham, aged 18 months, who became my special responsibility. Malcolm was born after I was advised to return to nursing. It is a constant joy to see how the children give their lives sacrificially. Elizabeth is now married to a doctor and a grandmother herself, and Jean, who loved to climb trees at bedtime, is now taking leadership with her husband for Initiatives of Change in Australia. Chris, who aged four loved the *Beano* to be read to him, is now an eminent Professor on the other side of the Atlantic. As Big Liz in this new family, I became known as 'Biggles', the then current popular children's storybook character.

Living with the McAll family did much for my mental, physical and spiritual health, and I owe them a deep debt of gratitude for the training I had there. As they endured four years as prisoners of war in China, I felt it a privilege to be asked to live in their home.

After my stay with the McAll family it was decided that I should take a refresher course, having been out of hospital for eight years. Dear Jessie Wright, Sister in Out Patients and Casualty, was still in Canterbury. "You are the most stupid woman I know," she shouted across a clinic of 200 patients, as I struggled to put VD patients' notes in alphabetical order. I was shaking so much I could not remember if 'R' came before 'K' or not. Her brilliant management during the war was recognised, and her greatest moment in gaining the MBE was to say to the taxi driver, "Buckingham Palace please."

It seemed useful to become a midwife, and knowing that my new heart-throb had an office in the East End, I applied to the London Hospital, doing two months in Whitechapel, followed by four months at Queen Mary's, Hampstead. Periodically Her Majesty visited when sisters were busy in the labour wards with no time to put on a clean apron, and she would say, "That tap was dripping the last time I was here." Her ladies in waiting knitted cot covers for our babies.

Relaxing before our final exam, watching slides in the sitting room of the Principal, one pupil midwife knocked over a lamp. "There goes another bit of Buck House," said Miss Beaulah. Leaving the beautiful London Hospital sister's uniforms, I began Part Two midwifery at Watford Maternity Hospital.

Regrettably, I cannot remember many of the patients I nursed. At gatherings with my midwife friends they spend the afternoon reminiscing about their patients, and I am sadly reticent, until recently when I found myself taking a computer course two desks away from the mother of triplets that I had delivered. We were delighted to see one another, as I have many photographs of her family, and one lovely coloured one appeared on the front of *The Nursing Mirror*. The children are qualified doctors in their thirties, living in Australia and elsewhere.

One memory I have is of a Sunday afternoon, being called out to a patient in Watford (Cassiobury Park). The mother was in advanced labour, and the GP and I sat at the bedside. She delivered her baby happily, and the doctor was about to finish the delivery when I grabbed the foetal stethoscope and said, "Excuse me, sir, I think there's another one there." So there was, and we had to improvise the baby's bath as an extra cot.

Left in charge of the Watford Maternity Hospital at night, I went off duty one morning, thinking that I had better read through the fire instructions. That night the resident doctor dropped a cigarette in the waste paper basket which caught fire in his bedroom next to the ward nursery. Fortunately, a father who was awaiting the birth of his baby fought the blaze with the doctor whilst I remembered instructions revised that morning. I called the fire engines and the men removed a blazing chair with not much further damage caused. The hospital committee were suitably grateful for my efforts, not least because of the danger to all the sleeping new-born babies.

When on duty, Matron slept above another part of the hospital. My job on occasions was to keep 17 babies quiet all night. It was difficult knowing that at any moment a little bedroom-slippered lady wearing a dressing gown would appear at the ward door, asking, "Can I have a sleeping tablet, nurse?" You knew then that your noisy charges had kept her awake; one discovered ways of coping with yelling babies!

One of our sisters, a very short little lady, loved football. One day I passed the local Watford football ground (quite close to our old maternity hospital) and was surprised to see her peering through a hole in the high wooden fence surrounding the noisy match in progress. She had a first-class view of the game and ascertained the score before returning on duty.

For many years as junior, I was put on 'nights' with a friend who was an immensely fast bed-maker. We seemed to whip around 50 beds at a rate of knots. If the neighbour's lawn mower had prevented our sleep that day, my reactions were rather slow. She did not pass her midwife teacher's exam (I'm not sure how I did), but went on to be Matron of the maternity hospital in Hobart, Tasmania, where she was very successful. She sent me some lovely calendars of the antipodes each year, begging me to go out to stay. Sadly she died recently, and I miss her regular Christmas gifts.

Before taking up midwifery, I nursed in Hampstead for a few months doing a refresher's course, working with Dr Toohey, the author of a well-known nurses' text book. He terrified most of the staff, but after my very strict training at Canterbury, I stood up to him, and I think he respected it.

One old lady had to be certified to go into a mental establishment, an experience which I hadn't had before. Her neighbour in the ward kindly finished embroidering a tray cloth I was struggling to make and she offered to 'tip me' when she left – something we could never accept, of course.

I still have a photo of the first baby I delivered on my own in the district. It was a lonely responsibility sitting all night wondering whether the patient should go into hospital, or if I could deliver the baby safely.

Before this I assisted at the delivery of a patient in Carpenter's Park. I do not think that my midwife (I was the pupil) was very experienced, and there was considerable haemorrhage on the sheets, which I had to wash in the patient's bath. We had sent for the 'flying squad' and the big white chief came to see what I was doing. "Enjoying your first delivery, Coxon?" asked the Honourable Eve Chetwynde MBE. "I'm so pleased to see you and the flying squad," I said. She was furious, and did not speak to me for weeks. She was a St Thomas' nurse and midwife, and being so capable she didn't realise how terrified I was at all the drama. When we were not busy we had to go to her little house in Watford to make-up her four-poster bed. When I finally passed my last midwife teacher's exam, she gave a party, and knowing that I did not drink, she told me that the punch was non-alcoholic. Unbeknown to me she had laced it with some strong spirit, and I could not understand why the room was going round!

We cycled to call-outs on our bikes, and some nights it was difficult to decide whether the baby would arrive before my junior nurse turned up with the gas and air – she had never used a bicycle at home in Africa.

Some midwives were billeted in the town, and I was sent to the home of Barrington Dalby, the famous BBC sports commentator and his wife. It was also a fascinating experience to be taken to meet famous broadcasters at Langham Place, such as Raymond Glendenning. His wife and I listened to 'Barry's' boxing and football commentary on the television. I recall her telling me that he would not eat his Christmas meal before working!

After a busy night on duty in the Midwifery department at Watford, a friend took me to St Albans Cathedral where Her Majesty presented the Maundy Money. It was an interesting occasion, but I could see little as I was behind a pillar, struggling to keep myself awake.

Becoming an examiner of the Central Midwives Board meant travelling to a number of hospitals and having a good lunch. One well known gynaecologist with me had a bad back, and instead of sharing the job of putting frightened pupil midwives through their paces, he sat back and chewed an aspirin. As a new girl to the job, I felt deeply responsible, especially as one came later to work in my midwifery department.

For many years I was able to attend MRA meetings and frequently took car and bus-loads of people to see plays at *The Westminster Theatre*. Good plays were put on week after week and we tried to fill the seats with folk from all over the country. Visiting East End homes to distribute tickets for these productions after working in hospital all day on the wards was a challenge. It was a privilege to go into homes in Poplar where I had worked as a midwife at the East End Maternity Hospital.

At weekends coach-loads would come from every corner of Britain to see the plays, which had a real message of hope and truth. They would stay with us in London (those of us near enough to offer accommodation), and then the following day we would all meet up again at the theatre for a rousing meeting, have lunch, and then our visitors would leave for Scotland, Ireland, Cornwall or other areas. It was a challenge to have complete strangers in our homes nearly every weekend but very rewarding.

On one occasion five visitors arrived and we had only four beds, so my mother slept on the kitchen floor. Months afterwards our Communist guests learnt of this and completely changed their ideology as a result.

One sunny day my mother asked me to take two old ladies to the Westminster Theatre – one was the nurse to the Queen of Greece. I drove down Bond Street and at the lights turned left into Piccadilly, wondering why the taxi alongside me stopped. A policeman on a motorbike overtook me as I drove round Eros, asking me why I had not stopped at the lights in Bond Street.

British Commonwealth Scholars – MRA friends after a presentation at St James' Palace in the presence of The Queen Mother, 1964

Summoned to Bow Street some weeks later, I explained to the lady on the bench that the sun dazzled me and I was a nurse on night duty. "Two pounds," she pronounced, and I returned to bed in Kingston Hospital, duly reprimanded.

The following Christmas the Superintendent Midwife was off duty and Matron told me that the Mayor was coming to see the Department early. However, we waited patiently as the babies became hungry and anxious mothers slipped out of bed and made their way to the nursery. That year it was the fashion for 'Baby Doll' night dresses. Suddenly there was an awful hush and in walked the Mayor and dignitaries with Matron. The mothers clutched screaming infants and sat on their beds, responding nervously to questions from the visitors. Later I received a severe ticking-off. "How could you let the Mayor see the mothers' knees?" said Matron. I was greatly sorry for myself, and when I finished duty I ran a deep bath and sat miserably until the phone suddenly rang in the nurses' home. Grabbing a towel I heard Matron's voice – "I have a ticket for *The Sleeping Beauty* at Covent Garden tomorrow night, would you like it?" All was forgiven.

Florence Nightingale wrote, "The very vastness of the work raises one's thought to God as the only one by whom it can be done. That is the solid comfort. He knows."

I was asked to write an essay on nursing in Britain, which enabled me to visit seven countries in Europe, and later I went to Spain for the International Conference of Midwives. I had won a coveted British War Memorial Scholarship. For three months I was able to observe hospitals and community work, sometimes actively looking after patients, and I enjoyed wonderful hospitality, seeing something of each region. The report of this visit is in the appendix.

It is St Luke's day as I write this chapter. The collect reminds us, "Almighty God, who inspired Luke the physician to proclaim the love and healing of Your son, give your Church, by the grace of the Spirit and through medicine of the gospel, the same love and power to heal through Jesus Christ, Our Lord."

Three Thousand Babies a Year

"If I fail the administration examination I shall need my bread and butter so I had better take the job of Midwifery Superintendent at Pembury Hospital for a year." That was my thinking 40 years ago. My mother joined me three years later in a house where I still live.

Pembury, previously an old work house, presented a challenge, as my predecessor was a brilliant midwife and administrator who won the MBE before sadly dying at an early age. Staff prefaced each remark by saying, "Miss H did this or that," until my morale was at rock bottom. We delivered 3,000 babies that year.

After much discussion with all our staff, we managed to have a new labour ward suite built. Then after a few words with one of our doctors who hunted with royalty, we had the delightful Duchess of Kent to open the brand new department. My management skills however had failed to win over an elderly Ward Sister who sat in her office whilst the Duchess visited each of her patients. My deputy was hastily given a pair of white gloves and did not know the names of any of the mothers.

25 years earlier the namesake of this royal visitor had come to see us at Canterbury. We asked one elderly patient on Bell Ward how he had enjoyed meeting her. "I could not hear a word, but she smelled something lovely," was his comment.

Reorganisation seems to be the name of the game in the NHS and I was invited to apply for a Nurse Training Officer's job covering 17 hospitals in 1970. Then began the happiest years of my career as I literally careered round hospitals in Kent, Sussex and London, when ultimately I had to work with 200 hospitals.

Opening of new Labour Ward, Pembury

Previously the Pembury maternity delivery rooms had been built with clear glass windows, allowing all visitors to observe babies coming into the world. Working nearby enabled us to rush to order frosted glass before the first patient arrived. Our pupil midwives were sent all over Kent with a variety of raincoats, caps and bicycles. On a day off I remembered that in Hertfordshire our Matron visited her district pupil midwives so I got in my little *Ford* and drove to see my nurse near Chatham. After the usual courtesies I drove off, but thought I should call at Kent County Hall to chat to my opposite number there. I was met by a furious head of district midwives, who stamped her foot saying, "How dare you come onto my patch." As I was shaking so much her deputy took me to the basement for a cup of coffee. She later became a very senior nurse in the NHS.

Driving as fast as I could back from Maidstone to Tunbridge Wells I confronted an equally angry lady in Matron's office. "Why did I go out of the district without permission?" even though I had gone at my own expense. A few months later the NHS began to unite Hospital and Community Services, but I had been too advanced in my approach.

Staff shortages and the threat, "You had better make a success of this job or else," threw me into a panic resulting in a few car crashes, but finally the new work training Nursing Auxiliaries in 17 hospitals was filmed on the evening TV news programme after our annual competition. I had to give a running commentary to the programme, which was not a happy experience, but unbeknown to me, one of the consultants had plied the programme makers with 'Bull's Blood' at lunch time, and everything seemed to slow down during the afternoon. Later Dennis Thatcher, the husband of the Prime Minister, gave the prizes away to the winning hospital. I had met him whilst practising chipping at Lamberhurst Golf Club in November 1974, and I chatted to him, asking him about how he enjoyed America from whence he had just returned. I was amazed that he agreed to give the prizes for our competition when I asked him, and he was extremely helpful.

Sadly the week before the television programme my mother had suddenly died as I came off duty. She had had a hip operation in Pembury and recovered well but afterwards I had to take some weeks off to nurse her.

Denis Thatcher at Nursing Auxiliaries Competition

Working at Leybourne Grange hospital I called in at lunchtime to ensure her carer had given her a meal. She wanted me to stay and said that the lunch was rather heavily spiced, but I was due at the Kent and Sussex Hospital in the afternoon. Returning home at 6.00 pm I thought the house seemed quiet. My very dearly loved mother had died when I was in hospital. Doctor Peter Waterfield came immediately but mouth to mouth resuscitation was useless. My sorrow at her death, alone in our house, still is with me today.

In retrospect I realise the wealth of wisdom my mother bequeathed to me and as I grow older I understand much that she fought for. Finding an old page she had written, I quote,

I have been asked to write a brief summary of my life. Why, I can't think, but it may interest a few people and the family who know me.

My parents who lived in Derby were married at St Andrew's Church and took a house in Litchfield Street, Burton-on-Trent. This was in 1886. I was born on September 19th 1888. My father, Ormsby Taylor, was a practising lawyer in the town. My mother was the daughter of Dr Carter Wigg MD and his wife, Maria, and they had three daughters – my mother, also Maria, who was the eldest, Constance and Emily. Two sons were Lancelot and Leslie. After two years my brother, Roland was born and we moved to a bigger house at 236 Branston Road. Two years after, my sister Nancy Adela was born, and when I was six years old I went to a local school. The next move was to a delightful country village, Barton-under-Needwood, four miles from Burton. 'Erisbeg' was a large house with four sitting rooms and ten bedrooms. The large garden had a field beyond where we had lovely hay parties and picnics for many of our young friends. After two years my sister Olive was born and two years after that my third sister Audrey arrived. We had a resident Governess, Miss Carter, two maids, a 'char' and a gardener. Miss Carter was rather grim but good hearted, and her sister Laura who used to help domestically came over.

When I was about ten years old and Nancy eight we both went daily by train to Litchfield High School (eight miles away) as in those days there were no cars, only carriages and pony carts. The Head Mistress (Miss Hawkins) was a splendid but austere head as was Miss Mason. Others included Miss Makin, Nancy's bete noir, and Miss Cruickshank, whom we all loved. When I was about 15, my parents decided to move back to Burton, and we took Peel House, eleven bedrooms and six sitting rooms and a large garden. The house was situated overlooking the big football ground. We had many friends with much entertaining.

Peel House was so called because Sir Robert Peel had lived there. We had many friends and a constant flow of visitors, especially for big matches as our large drawing room overlooked it. It was a popular attraction for guests and family. Music played a big part for we all learnt to sing and play. As my parents took part we decided to start a little Concert party. We called ourselves 'The Burton Barnstormers'. We became popular with many clergy and ministers who were glad to accept our help with short plays and music to help with parochial expenses. We decided to make our own costumes, originally Japanese then 'Happy Harvesters' with men in smocks and clogs and girls in sun bonnets – hay making clothes. Finally we decided on Canadian Mounties with stiff hats, pistols in our belts and the men had trousers with a fringe down the sides.

Dr Carter Wigg, Elizabeth's Maternal Grandfather

One of our party was someone we had known for some time, Fred Coxon to whom I got engaged. We were married at Burton Parish Church on

August 19th. It was a grand occasion and after a lovely Wedding Breakfast we went to Skegness for our honeymoon. We bought a little house on the Branston Road leading to Branston village where the *Branston Pickle* was made. Nancy, Olive and Audrey were my bridesmaids and Arthur Coxon (Fred's brother) officiated at our wedding with the Vicar of Burton. Arthur was then Vicar of Priors Lee in Shropshire and later became Rural Dean in Tamworth after years at Tunstall with a parish of 17,000 in the 'hungry 30s', in the Potteries.

Three years after, Elizabeth was born, and for three or four years Pom Sechiari an old friend lived with us at White Ley until the tragic passing of my beloved husband following a short illness in July 1927.

A few years before he died we bought a little bungalow at Wittering right on the sea which we all loved. During the war it was occupied by the army and razed to the ground – nothing remains now but the foundations.

The bungalow, 'The Three Bears', had three bedrooms, although afterwards we added another one, and we had visitors of all ages. Elizabeth joined a little pony club and learned to ride. After Fred had passed on I sold the bungalow and took a house at Bosham, eventually near Aunt Cossie, who had a house just opposite and we had many happy years there, till the war came.

Elizabeth took up work as there was need for agriculture, doing land work – milking and delivering the produce. She also took up dancing and drama which she enjoyed enormously, but overworked and had to relinquish all work for a time.

Mercifully she made a complete recovery and took a post of teaching elocution, dance and drama in Switzerland. I took a house at Golder's Green where I met friends in Moral Rearmament and Frank Buchman who inspired my heart and understanding of my real need of change, with a new light. All this was not easy to begin with but it brought a new sense of direction and produced a real peace of heart I had not known before.

After Elizabeth's time of teaching at Westonbirt School – with the war still raging – she decided to train in a medical field, and eventually took a degree at Kingston. It is an interesting situation as she has done remarkably well and I realise how many members of our family have earned important posts in the medical world.

Grandfather on mother's side was a doctor (Carter Wigg MD) and he wrote a number of articles on the work of midwifery, child birth and attending difficulties and dealing with associated problems.

My grandfather on my father's side was a qualified Veterinary Surgeon dealing with problems associated with sick animals.

Bishop of Rangoon, George West, and his wife
Grace,MRA friends who stayed with us

My father's eldest brother Seymour Taylor was a
specialist in throat and chest problems and practised
in Portman Square, London with a large clientele of
important people. He also wrote a book The *Index
of Medicine*. In a letter published in *The Daily
Telegraph* (April 9th 1969) it quotes "Taylor's
Medicine" sent by Florence Nightingale on June 19th
1895 from 10 South Street Park Lane to her friend.
Presumably the two must have known each other

(my uncle and Miss Nightingale lived comparatively near).

Another brother Ernest Taylor was a practising doctor in Norfolk so it is not surprising that Elizabeth should ultimately take to the medical profession. She is now (1974) in charge of the In-Service Training Department in Pembury Hospital, and as Group Nurse Training Officer for 17 hospitals has to arrange lectures, study groups for Auxiliary Nurses and women of all grades. Especially there is a need for many women who have had training before marriage to return to nursing. The scheme of course for 'Back to Nursing' is of utmost value.

I moved here to Pembury from a flat I had in Putney for six years and it is a real joy to be in real country and to have made many kind friends. At 85 I have so much to be thankful to God for, countless blessings day by day. W M Coxon, Family Reminiscences.

My mother's funeral took place on what would have been her 86th birthday, a brilliant sunny day, and so many friends and family came and enjoyed the cake planned for her anniversary.

A short time after my mother's death several nurses and I, together with an ex- missionary Orthopaedic Surgeon, were asked to do the morning 'Lift up your Hearts' radio programme for two weeks. My cousin at Rochester phoned to say he had heard my broadcast and gone back to sleep!

Ted

Whenever I met my aunts through the years, I always felt that they were saying, "Poor Elizabeth – still not married." All of them having married successfully, they often dropped comments such as, "She is quite attractive," whenever my younger cousins got married one after another. However, a miracle occurred!

The stress of constant changes in the National Health Service precipitated me into a job visiting 17 hospitals (later 200) in the Southeast of England. I was constantly crashing my car, or someone else's (on one occasion my male tutor's).

In the village a garage came to my rescue on a number of occasions. Ted Taylor, a brilliant retired engineer, was helping out. He was also caring for his wife, who was desperately ill with cancer. Sadly his wife died in very distressing circumstances after treatment in Guy's Hospital and soon after this my mother also died.

One day a couple of years later, I noticed (after yet another accident) that Ted gave me a 'funny look'. When I needed someone to try out the car after a problem, he offered with alacrity, and somehow we drifted into the occasional outing in the bluebell woods. After about eighteen months of seeing each other, Ted proposed to me – I was 60 years old, nine years his junior. Initially I said no, but more requests followed at regular intervals.

One Wednesday I had to have my hearing tested at the Kent and Sussex Hospital, and having been advised not to drive home, I asked Ted to come and fetch me. As I sat down, somewhat woozy after treatment, he made me a cup of tea and gave me his usual gift of a large box of chocolates. Proposing yet again, he said that he could not stand it, and must have a positive answer by the weekend.

As Ted took himself home, I rang two families – the vicar of Mark Cross, Alan Thornhill, and Dr Paul Campbell, and their wives, asking if I could come over to see them. We all listened to God, and their thought was to ask me what guidance I had received. In their retirement home at Rotherfield, the Thornhills said, "Whatever God says to you, we will support you in your decision." I told them that my thought from God was to marry Ted.

On Saturday Ted drove me to help edit an education paper we were producing with friends. At coffee time I escaped to visit my friend Dr Paul Campbell and his wife Annejet. Again, I was asked what God had told me to do, and I told them that I felt it was right to marry Ted. They also offered their support of my decision.

At 5.00 pm Ted came to collect me in my car and I said, "The answer is yes." I thought that he would collapse in the road, such was his elation. As we drove home I decided we could tell my companions and take them out to dinner to celebrate.

One thing tipped the scales for me to accept Ted's offer of marriage. My work at David Salomen's house in Southborough was near his home in Speldhurst. After an exhausting day organising a course of Senior Health Authority personnel I ran down the hill to his home as he had said that he was not well. It was late, and I did not want to disturb him. I peeped through the curtain-less kitchen window, and my heart turned over as I saw him sitting by the fire looking so sad and woebegone. I realised that I really loved him and wanted to help him.

Working full time and preparing for my wedding was exhausting, and on the morning of the actual day I remember lying down on the drawing room carpet worn out. In between my job as a Training Officer in 200 hospitals, my wedding outfit was bought during coffee and lunch breaks three miles away in Tunbridge Wells. Dear Mrs Penn altered the dress from *Weeks*, now *Hoopers*, lengthening it and adding a pink under skirt to the grey lace outfit, and a hat was discovered in the attic having done service at Christ's Hospital for Speech Day. Somehow it all came together as I struggled with invitations, but horror of horrors suddenly, a few days before 'The Day', a stone from my engagement ring went missing. The garden, my office, the house, the car and every place visited recently was searched. As I opened the book with names of wedding guests, panic over – nestling in the binding was my cherished jewel.

The Happy Couple

With the bridesmaids, Gina and Julie Hollamby (my step-
granddaughters), and parents Ian and Jenifer

Wedding Reception

The first notes of the Wedding March played by the dear elderly village organist Rex Turner enabled my cousin Vanessa Faulkner's husband David to propel me up the aisle, and Ted and I managed to get through the service without mishap thanks to the wonderful help of Rev Alan Thornhill, who took the service beautifully. Having played for other brides I know the agony as relations and friends sit through repetitions of the organist's repertoire as young beautiful brides keep every one waiting.

The reception at the *Calverley Hotel* in Tunbridge Wells where my Aunt Edythe had spent the previous night is a blur in my mind except Dr Ken McAll reminding the guests of my dancing in the hospital wards with bedpans, at Canterbury during the war, something I had completely forgotten. Ken's wife Frances came to stay with me and supported me more than I can ever say through the last 50 years.

Ted and I drove, after a wonderfully warm send-off from our guests, to the *Hilton Hotel* in Hayward's Heath. The day after, we made steady progress to the west of England, calling on friends and family until, after an exceedingly cold hotel we arrived at Minehead where I had to buy a warm anorak. Fortunately Lynmouth produced a delightful hotel on the hill above the scene of the disastrous floods a few years previously. Here we could at last relax as our room overlooked the ever-changing sea. I cannot remember the reason but we had our first quarrel in Clovelly, soon to be resolved. A bossy nurse had to learn quickly to say sorry. Certainly the next nine years were the happiest in my life.

As Ted and I had our own houses it was difficult to amalgamate our belongings, and it became quite a frequent shout from the kitchen if one of us were washing up, "I've broken another of your cups," as we struggled to unite our household goods and lives. When Ted died I abandoned things like the toaster, the fountain in the garden pond, tape recorders and ciné films, because they all went wrong and I couldn't mend them.

When Ted and I got married in 1980, I had many adjustments to make, not least in trying to keep up with Ted's many hobbies. I had no knowledge of cars or mechanical vehicles - apart from being able to drive my own *Ford* and ride a midwife's bicycle. I certainly could not shoot, but I soon learned to handle a pistol and gun.

Ted sold his house and joined me in Pembury, and we had to put up extra sheds to house all his tools and motorbikes. Ted worked hard in the garden and house and later he carried on part-time at *Rawson's Garage*. When I retired from the National Health Service I was able to help in local village and church organisations.

Learning to rifle shoot on my stomach at the local Tunbridge Wells rifle club took much concentration and many 'Bosh Shots'. However it made a change from rushing round wards in a starched apron.

Camping, another first, was an eye-opener. The camping site at Abergavenny, just over the border of Wales, seemed to qualify for the longest and wettest grass field, through which we had to visit the wash room.

Married life gave me a taste of freedom and in spite of my many cookery failures, enabled me to be a person in my own right. At 60 years of age I was not just an appendage of a profession or a movement. However it was a privilege to be asked to become a school Governor, not only of Christ's Hospital but also of Pembury Primary School which had 400 children.

Ted continued with his many interests and some new ones. The Graham Walker Memorial Run round Beaulieu in the New Forest (26 miles), organised by the Sunbeam Motorcycle Club, gave him great happiness and satisfaction. He also made regular appearances at the Vintage Motor Cycle gatherings at Tinkers Park (Hadlow Down) near Heathfield, and elsewhere.

Ted loved to watch sports of every kind on television - golf, bowls, cycling, running, car and motorcycle racing - in many of which he had achieved much himself. He was always full of fun and quick-witted jokes. How much he gave of himself to others in spite of pain and, latterly, a dull diabetic diet. He was a perfect husband, considerate, kind, helpful and always interested. How cross he would be if people said they were bored.

Letters came from all over the world from people asking his advice. He was the expert on the *Brown* make of motorbike. Out of his past experiences, he replied to all the letters.

Stone deaf for the latter part of his life, Ted spent much time in silence. However, with increasingly improved hearing aids, he loved his music tapes, especially those of brass bands, Jimmy Shand and Mantovani. His son John had given him some of the tapes. Ted would play the same tunes over and over again. He was a wonderfully peaceful man. He did not like pious 'blather'; he just loved God and his life exemplified the joy of living.

Ted took up bowls late in life, with his characteristic enthusiasm and sportsmanship. He had a good eye, but a bad knee.

As a member of the committee of the Tunbridge Wells and St Peter's Shooting Club, Ted took on more and more responsibility for the Pistol and Rifle Sections. He began coaching young beginners, while continuing to participate in regular weekly and monthly matches himself. A number of people remember his training sessions; at least one trainee reached the Olympics.

Bisley is to shooting what Wimbledon is to tennis, and in 1985 we spent a week there in an enormous marquee. Ted marked the score cards which came in every thirty minutes. I learnt the hard way how to file the results in huge trays. There were 4,000 competitors from all over the world. Rifle shooting - pistol shooting - everything except bows and arrows! Ted had to check the shot holes in the cards. This was essential as in one Olympic competition our leading woman lost marks because she fired a cross shot on to someone else's target.

If people felt they had been incorrectly marked, they paid 75p and challenged the judges. Their target was scrutinised by the Secretary of the National Rifle Association, who sat with us in the marquee all day to see fair play. If the competitor was right he got his money back and the mathematicians had to start all over again adding up totals and seeing who was due for prizes.

We filed and filed until my back would hardly hold me up. But it was such fun. To see the bronzed muscular chaps come in kicking themselves if they got a bad score, or rushing in to see their team results, was most rewarding.

Most clubs and committees have their own tents with their flags. The whole acreage of Bisley is covered with tents and caravans, along with the permanent buildings for well-known clubs such as the Royal Artillery.

Long distance competition, about three-quarters of a mile, required special skills, not least because the targets can scarcely be seen without looking through a magnifying glass on the gun. As the shots rung out a soldier used to run from one end of the target to the other (below ground), putting up scores - black patches in shot holes. Some competitors favoured lying on their backs for this long-distance shooting – Ted also preferred this position. Ted had shot for Kent and was one of the distinguished company of people who got a score of 400 out of 400.

The Vintage Motorcycle Club Ltd.

OFFICIAL
PROGRAMME   **BP**   PRICE 10/-
(50p)

FESTIVAL OF 1000 BIKES

at BRANDS HATCH
Sunday, 26th August, 1984

Organised by the West Kent Section - V.M.C.C.

Regular features include:
News of the month
Reports on all Big Events
Readers Letters
Mini-manuals
Road Test Reprints
Wheelin' 'n' Dealin'
Book Reviews
Classified Ads.

The CLASSIC MotorCycle

Published every month   **20/-**

In 1984 we went to the Festival of 1,000 Bikes at Brands Hatch. Ted was given a lap of honour on his beloved *Brown*, bringing cheers from the spectators. I remember his name being called on the loudspeaker - he then disappeared plus the *Brown* into the pit. To my horror I saw an ambulance move in. Were my worst fears to be realised? No - there was Ted helmeted and cheerful, merrily doing his first lap. Then he went round a second time. He was presented with a splendid trophy, after which he came out and gave it to me as I sat in the stands. It was the proudest moment of my life.

I remember deafening sounds of motorbikes from all over the world revving up as we arrived in our caravan, with me clutching the bike to stop it falling over. We had entertained a couple at home the previous night who had biked (she on pillion) from Montreux the day before. Thanks to friends at the Caux conference whom Ted had met, he visited our Swiss biking enthusiasts, as he did folk in Holland when enjoying the Dutch motorbike festival.

As mentioned already, each year Ted went to Beaulieu for the Graham Walker Run in the New Forest on vintage motorbikes. Graham Walker's widow presented the cups of merit, and her son, Murray Walker, the famous TV presenter, was very helpful to me, announcing my book over the tannoy at Brighton following the London to Brighton run the year after Ted's death.

A local 'garden' run by Ted was 25 miles round local Kent lanes. The one I remember most clearly was the hop farm at Beltring, at the time belonging to the brewers *Whitbread*, and the stabling for the dray horses used for drawing the Lord Mayor's coach for the November show in London.

Ted continued to participate in the annual Pioneer Run to Brighton. In 1985 *Epsom and Ewell Herald* reported:

Despite hailstones and thunder, more than 300 of the world's oldest motorcycles left Epsom Downs on Sunday for the annual Pioneer Run.

Bound for Brighton, the pre-World War I bikes and hardy riders set out from Tattenham Corner for the toughest test of the year. Hundreds had gathered to cheer the veterans on their way.

Epsom's Mayor and Mayoress, Councillor Norma Fryer and her mother, waved them off... First away, under the Mayor's flag at 8.30 am was Ed Taylor from Tunbridge Wells on his 1909 three-and-a-half horse-powered *Brown*.

The honour was his because he had done the run the most number of times.

In 1986 Ted had a wonderful Dutch Run in Holland, where he gained the trophy for the oldest Rider and Bike (combined ages) - a beautiful Delft plate which he treasured greatly.

In the Pioneer Motor Cycle run of 1987 Ted wore vest number one. He was the oldest member on the oldest motorcycle, and was sponsored by members of St Peter's Church, Pembury, to raise money for the Church. He also was given the Sunbeam Motor Cycle Club's Golden Jubilee award for completing the most Pioneer Runs since 1903.

A few yards from the finish a car came out from a side road. Ted tried to avoid it, but the vehicles collided and Ted lay in the road, thinking that his leg was broken. The *Brown* was pushed to the finish by willing hands, while Ted was taken by ambulance to Brighton Hospital. After treatment he was sent home to Pembury that night. Our faithful friend Stuart Cosham drove us both back in the much-loved *Volkswagen*, with the damaged *Brown*.

Ted had physiotherapy for the injured knee in Pembury Hospital and was offered an operation on the other knee, which had given pain for some years. This was to take place on our return from a visit we were about to make to the Far East.

The *Brown* was sold at Sotheby's and given to the National Motor Cycle Museum, Birmingham, where it is on display, together with all the medals associated with it. After the terrible fire at the museum in 2003 I was relieved to learn that his bike and medals were not damaged.

In 1981 we visited Ted's son John and family in Hong Kong and had an opportunity to get to Macau and into China. Among other interesting visits we saw the house of Dr Sun Yet Sen, and the children's school dedicated to his memory.

During this visit it was a delight to stay with John and Wendy and to meet their children Karen and Simon. Karen, Ted's granddaughter, now has an important job in the Ministry of Health, and Simon is an architect. In their 12th floor flat we watched the planes coming in to the airport, almost lower than the balcony on which we were standing.

As I was still working in the NHS, The Royal College of Nursing arranged for me to see some hospitals and to go out with district nurses. The Christian Hospital in Hong Kong was in the capable hands of European administration. Matron's office faced a huge slope of concrete to prevent the high buildings from slipping down the hill. This had happened to skyscrapers in previous years.

In Hong Kong a district nurse showed me the squalid wooden shacks she had to visit, telling the relatives to fetch her from the bottom of the hill as there were no roads or signposts among the chaotic wooden huts. Hundreds of boats were anchored in the bays, and patients suffering from burns (a common occurrence) needed their nurse to step from boat to boat in order to attend to their injuries.

Hong Kong slums

Marks and Spencer's employed Chinese folk near the harbour and many goods were sent to Britain. For years I could send *M&S* tokens to the family knowing they could be redeemed at the same value.

Ted and I then made our way into China, staying for a night in Macau and visiting, but not playing, the tables of the casino. Very strict rules had to be observed as we crossed into China; we looked out over miles of barbed wire with gun-carrying soldiers every few yards along the borders with the free world.

Put into a new bus, made in China, we were taken past acres of fields growing food for the millions living in Hong Kong. As the women stood up to their thighs in mud they passed buckets of earth etc, in much the same the way as we were taught to tackle fires with stirrup pumps in World War II. Domestic washing of clothes was carried out in streams nearby. To my amazement our bus driver heard me talking about hospitals and kindly (and illegally) took us both round some back streets to see the hospital of that city, an unpainted unprepossessing building with a run-down set of benches outside on a balcony for patients. On the window ledge behind were a collection of filthy thermos flasks containing prescribed medicines for outpatients.

We returned to our bus through a maze of thousands of bicycles but we managed to photograph the father of a delightful chubby baby. How I wish we could have sent him the snap of his 18 month little boy. Other people were reluctant to have their photos taken and hid their faces or scowled as we passed. Many looked at our bus as if we had come from the moon.

> Civilisation that has grown up intellectually and industrially must grow up intellectually and spiritually or perish.
>
> Peter Howard, who was at prep school with my uncle, Geoffrey Coxon.

Back in England, and as a step great grandmother, I had the joy of meeting more of Ted's family and was able to attend Julie and Terry's wedding at St James' Church in Tunbridge Wells. My step great granddaughters are Lauren, Jodie and Amy.

Ted and I went again to Hong Kong early in 1989 and had another happy visit. All the family came to see us off at the hotel and we joined the tour bus to the airport and so to Singapore. As we got off the plane the heat hit us, as it does when we go into a very hot bathroom after being out on the coldest English evening in December.

Ted was determined to visit the Bird Sanctuary which John had told us about, and also to see the beauty of the orchids for which Singapore is so famous.

A great friend in the Pembury Women's Institute had arranged for us to spend the evening with her son and his wife. He was a Managing Director of the Hong Kong Bank in Singapore. We listened to the monkeys chattering in the garden as we sipped our drinks and phoned our host's mother in Pembury. While Ted dozed off peacefully we talked of local village news back in England before walking round the magnificent swimming pool in the garden.

The hotel in which we were staying was built on land previously owned by Wendy's family. A magnificent collection of shops was also built on the family land. We had four days in Singapore and then went to Bangkok, where we met friends of David and Margot Young. As we went out to dinner with these new friends, sitting on the floor to watch the exquisite Thai dancers, Ted was beginning to tire. Always cheerful, always interested, he was courteous to the end.

The next day I went on a bus tour round Bangkok while Ted had a quiet morning resting. After a light lunch we sat and watched the fascinating water traffic on the river. I had been up at 6.30 am to watch the Buddhist monks on the terrace as they were given breakfast by the hotel staff after the religious ceremony held outside.

During the afternoon Ted and I sat quietly. I sketched a little. At dinner we decided we would celebrate our wedding anniversary - nine years and one week. Ted complained of pain and we struggled to get him up to our room before he collapsed. A doctor was called in, then the ambulance which took him to hospital. At 2.00 am Ted passed away peacefully. The English-speaking staff at the Adventist hospital allowed me to stay with him in the Intensive Care Unit until the end. I was then allowed to stay in the empty ward until morning. There was a Gideon Bible, English on one side and Thai on the other, which helped to preserve my sanity. Ted's death brought out so much love, care and concern in the Thai people, both in the hospital and the hotel.

Ted had bought me a wooden reproduction of the beautiful Thai vessels in which we had been served our meal the previous night. It was a minute replica of the bowls for rice, meat and other dishes, on a tiny tray.

He was always so generous in showering his family and friends with numberless gifts. Every time he went on holiday he bought treasures, some of which were kept for the next birthday or Christmas presents.

How I miss Ted's love and generosity. How little did I recognise his immense love and caring - something I had never experienced during my whole life. This was a tremendous privilege - words cannot express my grief which will be with me as I remember him all the days of my life.

Ted's daughter Jennifer flew immediately from Tunbridge Wells, also his son John from Hong Kong. Ted was cremated the next day in blazing sunshine in a Temple (Buddhist and Hindu), the only cremation facilities in Bangkok. A warm-hearted Australian clergyman took the Christian Service - competing with Buddhist prayers broadcast over very loud speakers. The festival of water-throwing was in progress as children, Buddhist monks and many others took part in their own services held just near ours.

We released Ted, as a family, to one of the enormous ovens in the temple, and each of us threw in a taper to start the fire. His son said afterwards how his father would have loved to photograph the ceremony! An enormous wreath of orchids from the hotel where we were staying accompanied Ted, and the other flowers went to the minister's own church.

A Service of Thanksgiving for the life of Edward Leslie Taylor was held at St Peter Upper Church, Pembury, on 2nd May 1989. His ashes were interred in Pembury Cemetery following the service.

Life after Ted

After Ted's death I was asked to help the children at Pembury Primary School with their reading. The headmaster (whom I later put forward for the MBE) came and said it might help me in my bereavement, and as a Governor I loved every Monday afternoon, sitting with dozens of children two or three at a time and helping them to read. I learnt much of the modern textbooks that were being read by seven-year-olds, but above all I learnt about the village families. One little girl said at the end of the summer term, "I'm going to be a bridesmaid next week to my mummy, and the following week bridesmaid to my daddy." It was heart-breaking, but we are still in touch, and she has two lovely children. As a Governor I was asked to help the Kent Association for Under Elevens, and worked at Kent County Hall with Lester Betts. Our committee produced *Legs Eleven*, a booklet following on other publications for children under the age of eleven. The following amusing quotation appeared in the front of the book:

Today's youth is rotten to the core,
it is evil, godless and lazy.
It will never be what youth used to be,
and it will never be able to preserve our culture.

Babylonian Clay Tablet
3,000 Years Old

A light-hearted handbook for Parents

LEGS ELEVEN

Edited by Lester Betts

We also spent many hours at Swattenden near Cranbrook helping young refugees, aged 11-16, from all over the world. Many were unable to speak English, and our job was recognised by the Tunbridge Wells Mayor with a certificate. The whole project was largely initiated by the very hard work of Hazel Hawes-Richards.

Having delivered mothers (and in some cases grandmothers) of these little ones in Pembury Hospital, it was a privilege to care for the next generation, and the village responded by opening their hearts in hospitality when I asked them to care for our Russian choir, having them to stay in their houses. Even when we had to take our visitors from St Petersburg to perform at the annual prestigious Brighton Festival they returned to their Pembury hostesses.

Sudden bereavement is always devastating but a friend, knowing my interest in music, asked for help in publishing some Christian children's songs translated from Scandinavian languages and previously produced in Helsinki by the talented musician Margareta Othman-Sundell. We formed a committee and enlisted the Patronage of the Bishop of Rochester, The Finnish Ambassador and Miss Ann Widdecombe MP.

As the songs were put on tape, using well-known European singers, we managed to play it to the translator the day before he died. With help from Kent County Council we printed the songs and distributed tapes and CDs throughout the world. All the proceeds were sent to support the Russian Children's Hospital at St Petersburg through the Komso Children's Hospital Charity.

An additional bonus was the magnificent concert given by the Sackville Singers in Pembury Upper Church. The programme included some of our songs.

Faced with financing this project, I gathered some good friends in the village – Mother's Union folk like Jean Aust, ex-China Inland Mission friends at Cornford House (Margaret and Mary Weller), Wendy Carter and other MRA friends. In London Bill Cameron-Johnson, the brilliant artist, agreed to join Tony Matthews the chairman of governors at Pembury School, Tony Thomas, Colin and Maureen Wookey, Francis Brown, Margaret Thompson, Margaret Jackson and others at Greencoat Place (the headquarters of MRA in London after the sale of the Westminster Theatre). Having enjoyed the support of Lester Betts, a Kent County

Councillor, we approached the Kent County Print firm and ordered 2,500 copies of the songs.

In a series of miracles, we had discovered a firm of musical professionals in the lovely Sussex village of Blackboys, near Heathfield. Once we had obtained the words and music, written and devised by Margaret Othman-Sundell from Helsinki, and translated into English, I drove over and found the marvellous company deep in the Sussex downland who had machines that produced copies of the music ready for mass printing. I remember the times Ted and I spent days at the fields nearby with his 1909 motorbike. Each year we camped in our caravan during the Hadlow Down Festival of ancient steamrollers, old cars, motorbikes, hot air balloons and dozens of exciting stalls. Ted had to do several rounds on his bike in demonstration of its ability to be ridden from London to Brighton each year.

To return to the publication of our children's songs, once printed the songs, together with expertly created CDs and tapes (1,000 of each), had to be sold and distributed around the world. Again friends as well as our committee helped in suggesting firms that would do this job – at a price! Some friends used computers to create stick-on address labels, and in every paper or magazine I could use I advertised that these lovely songs were available. Kent County Council education authorities allowed us to distribute the songs to primary schools throughout the county.

I subsequently visited Finland to finalise the publication of the Children's Songs and met Margaret Othman-Sundell's husband and many friends who offered generous hospitality. When we were invited by the Finnish Ambassador to a brilliant concert at the Embassy in England it was suggested that the proceeds of the songs went to help finance a children's hospital in Russia. Fortunately one of our committee, Tony Sursham, had met a doctor at the Children's Hospital in St Petersburg and, during an Easter visit, delivered our money personally. This was used to repair the buildings by a splendid team from Britain, the Komso Children's Charity headed up by Ken Harper.

After Ted died I also became involved in a number of charitable activities. Thanks to the generosity of Wendy and Dick Carter, we used their home, Matfield Court, to hold an Open Day raising money for Foundations of Freedom, a newly formed scheme for people aged 20-30 who had leadership potential. This had been set up on an international basis, and these young people from Eastern

Europe could return to their own country to implement what they had learned. Pembury Afternoon WI provided ploughman's lunches, and the village scouts erected a splendid marquee where stalls sold a wide variety of goods. John Faber, who had recently returned from the Czech Republic, gave an address and said he had met many people asking for help. We raised £700. The local press said we were raising cash for democracy.

Another set of friends took aid to Croatia, Rumania and Chernobyl, and made dozens of journeys to Russia. Tony Budell's life and marriage was in tatters when, one day, sitting in despair, he heard a voice saying, "I have work for you to do," and he felt sure it was from the Lord. He married Valerie and together they have worked unceasingly helping others. He has now been ordained as a church minister.

I managed to collect medical products from the organisation 'Echo' run by a doctor who, having previously worked in the Congo as a missionary, lived in our Golders Green home with his wife and two daughters. We were able to provide valuable drugs and medical equipment which could be taken to Eastern Europe by Tony Budell and his friends. Previously the terrible grief I experienced after my dear husband's death was helped by an invitation to Poland as a result of a chance meeting of a Polish singer at a wedding in the village. After Communism the world wondered, "What next?" Many people watched anxiously as eastern European countries struggled to emerge from the ruins of harsh regimes.

Invited to stay in the homes of Polish Christian friends, I was privileged to attend the annual City Folk Festival in Jaslo which hosted an MRA Music Conference on the theme, "Music - for a change in people and nations". It had been initiated by a journalist, Malgorzata Rudnicka, and concerts and sessions were held in the City Hall of Culture attended by the Mayor and other senior officials. Lord Mayhew, then our local MP, sent a warm letter to the opening occasion which I had to present. Unfortunately the Polish system of simultaneous translation was not working and I stood on the platform looking very silly as my belated speech was slowly translated, first into Russian, and then into Polish. I also forgot how to say "Good Morning" in Polish to the Senator, Kazimir Poniatowski.

Experts on the music of Poland and Lithuania described its role in national identity throughout their history, when people could not otherwise express their spiritual culture. An audience of musicians from Russia, Sweden, Canada, Belgium and elsewhere listened with interest to stories of change. Fifty of the visitors from Lithuania, Ukraine and Belorussia had their accommodation and food paid for by the Jaslo citizens.

The afternoon session was received with much interest when I showed a MRA video and played Margareta Othman-Sundell's Finnish children's songs. In the evening the Jaslo Music School gave a superb concert. While meetings were held, the Swedish violinists entertained us if there was a gap in the programme.

The whole weekend was taken up by a festival, so our concerts were in the main town hall, whilst simultaneously local groups of folk dancers and musicians were performing on a stage outside the hall in the streets. During our sessions intriguing folk tunes filtered through open doors as we listened inside to long speeches. Whenever possible we watched the dancing teams from villages competing, dressed in magnificent national costumes, reminding me of our Friday classes in Earls Court before the war, as we performed a Polonaise by Chopin in our long red boots. *Jaffa Cakes*, *Coca-Cola*, and orange juice were on the tables in front of us.

Inside the building we listened to an Egyptian composer, and then the haunting melodies of a Ukrainian Jewess. Both women had given each other a hug of reconciliation. A wonderful musical drama was performed by 30 young people from Harmony Theatre, St Petersburg. Those coming from Russia were filled with apprehension about being accepted by Poland, but by the end of the week they had made firm friends.

Returning by bus to Warsaw with the Russian Children we gave them supper before they went on to St Petersburg. Wiesiek and Marzena Kecik, with whom I stayed in Warsaw, had been recently in prison during the uprising. My hostess's mother was still alive but paralysed from being beaten in Siberia, her mind was still alert, nevertheless.

Visiting the ghastly exhibition of the Holocaust in Warsaw with my Jewish friend brought home to me the horror of half a million Jews murdered in one small area of that city. Eastern Europeans speak from their hearts. I was grateful to people in my church who enabled me to take food and clothing to Poland.

During the next days I was taken to see the amazing buildings of Warsaw rebuilt since the war. At the Institute of Jewish Historical Culture, a young Russian Jewish singer, Nadya, took me to meetings and to see memorabilia in their museum of the ghettos. Everyone gave tremendously warm welcomes and in spite of their poverty opened their hearts and homes to us.

The 30 Russian children with whom we travelled from Jaslo to Warsaw by bus ended the evening singing 'Holy Night'. A number of us from all over the world joined in singing in our own language – an example of unity for which Christians had prayed for many years. The children, some of whom came to stay with us afterwards, left after we had given them a hurried supper straight from the freezer, and travelled on to St Petersburg and a future which needs our prayers.

The ten years after Ted's death, filled as they were with our activities in Poland, Russia and Finland, were duly recorded in local papers.

One high spot was the visit to the Finnish Embassy and the splendid concert in our village church by the Sackville singers conducted by Anthony Dawson – graced by the presence of the Tunbridge Wells Mayor, Mayoress and other dignitaries. One good friend biked many miles in the pouring rain to help with the welcome to visitors – many sacrifices were made to enable us to send the proceeds to the Regional Children's Hospital in St Petersburg. The programme included several of the songs by Margaret Othman-Sundell. I should like to record my thanks to the vicar, Stephen Sealy and the PCC, for all their help with the concert.

The visit previously of the Russian Youth Choir had won the hearts of people in the village. They not only sang in the Victoria Precinct, Tunbridge Wells, making a great impression in the national costumes, but then were invited to Finchcocks in Goudhurst where they were filmed by the Finnish TV – the result was shown on Scandinavian programmes in Helsinki and elsewhere in Finland. Father Fortunato of the Russian Orthodox Church in London and other distinguished English people gave a tremendous welcome to the singers, who made a recording of their programme thanks to Dr Stephen Coles in Tudeley Church.

Fortunately there was much interest and I was asked to lecture to various church groups and WIs – this together with proceeds of my organist's fees helped to pay for expenses for the choir and later publication costs. The report I wrote following our visit to Poland in June 1992 can be found in the appendix to this book.

Visit of Russian Choir from Gatchina at Mascalls School

Russian Choir at Finchcocks

Family Matters

Mary Stollard, a much-loved aunt on my father's side, wrote for 'every paper in Britain' as I was told, and she was an outstanding historian on the Brontes. Linton Andrews (educated at Christ's Hospital) editor of the *Yorkshire Post* was a great friend of Mary's. She kept in touch with all our family with carefully written letters in clearly legible but very tiny lettering. I owe a debt to her for her interest in writing, but have not her memory of all the family activities.

It is essential to express my gratitude to all my cousins, first, second, and 'once removed' whatever that means. Since Ted's sudden death I have paid visits, spent hours on the telephone receiving loving therapy and making myself at home in their homes They have all become very close to my heart.

Westgate on Sea, Rowena Court – Elizabeth and Winifred Coxon, Barbara Stretton-Burgis, Mary Stollard, Bessie Chamberlain and dog

My step family have been amazingly supportive with constant hospitality in their homes in spite of their very busy lives. This, together with generous presents on many occasions, has helped the pain of bereavement to lessen after my husband's death.

Having been informed by my long-suffering publisher that another 2,500 words would be acceptable I feel the most important information has been left to the last. You, my reader, you are the objective of this book.

Daphne Coyne, my close cousin who wrote a fascinating account of her time in the WRNS, which is now in the Imperial War Museum, has a phenomenal memory of our family having closely observed them. She has been an unbelievable therapist as I have phoned her constantly since Ted died – her listening ear never failed. John Owen, her brother, supported me in the war, turning up for hospital dances, and after the war produced friends as partners for May week balls when he was at Keble College and I nursed on Nuffield ward at the Radcliffe Hospital.

Daphne and John Owen (cousins)

Daphne and Mick's son, Christopher, I remember as a delightful red-headed toddler when I stayed with them in Tunbridge Wells long before I ever thought of working there nearly 20 years later. Richard, their younger son, was a great help by showing how he produced tapes of his musical concerts in Dorset when I struggled to publish our choir from St Petersburg and later the Finnish Children's Songs. Sue, his wife a constant friend, gave me a wonderful weekend at Parnham House, where Viscount Lindley learnt so much of his skills of carpentry. She used her considerable talents in charge of catering there and later in a senior administrative position in Dorset.

Pat Read

Pat Read née Prince has provided me with days of wonderful holidays, feeding me like the proverbial turkey cock and driving me around Devon to visit the Read and the Faulkner families. After her busy life as an overworked wife of a vicar, with a hectic life teaching gym and games, she is now left with time to enjoy hours walking over Dartmoor and being involved in the letterbox activity, hiding and finding messages from many other enthusiasts. A talented musical family, both sons were in the Exeter Cathedral choir; she continues to enjoy singing in local concerts.

Nicolas, a busy GP in Sidmouth, with an equally busy wife, Monica, manage the three lovely children brilliantly (Sebastian, Anna and Isabel) and write their Christmas letters full of exciting holiday news. Clare his sister, now with Stan, her husband lives in Stratford-upon-Avon with two children, Sophia Joanna and Benjamin Dominic. Philippa Halls, the other sister is an editor of a North Devon paper, married to a very talented chef, Colin, with two little ones (Olivia Rachael and Luke Alexander), but I have not yet managed to visit them.

My Godson Simon, a freelance publisher, has just moved to Northleach and it was fun having the two small children (Daniel Oliver and Julianne) to stay in spite of appalling gales, with their Canadian mother, Kathryn, who is able to visit the grandparents on a regular basis with all the family. Sadly our other cousin Richard Taylor, one of the producers of the original *Chitty Chitty Bang Bang*, died, but his wife June has settled in Paris near her daughter Caroline Bouché with her French husband Guy and two teenage daughters, Clara and Manon. I was delighted to visit them in Paris in February 2004.

We seem to meet the Woodiwiss family at weddings and funerals – however, Heather and her husband were very hospitable when they lived near Folkstone. I miss them now they are in Lincolnshire. Colin, a distinguished architect, lives with his family in London, and Roger, who had a very senior position in the army in the Middle East, lives near Oxford. Both chat on the phone from time to time.

Simon's Graduation

As I write this I eagerly await a visit from my uncle and Godfather's grand daughter Nica Coxon, now at university in Nottingham. Tom, her brother I remember at the age of 10 playing football in Tamworth on the coldest day imaginable. He too is at university (I was never clever enough to go there). Julian their father worked with the Samaritans for 22 years – a splendid record.

My Aunts
Clockwise – Nancy, Winifred, Olive and Audrey

Geoffrey, a half-brother of my father and Uncle Arthur, married Enid Smith, and Vanessa their daughter married David Faulkner a farmer who had a marvellous herd of cows at Ide Hill near Sevenoaks where Uncle Geoffrey was Bank Manager of *Lloyds Bank*. Amongst other things, my uncle raised money for the new Maternity Wing of the local hospital. When it was to be opened by Winston Churchill's daughter, Mrs Soames, there were no mothers or babies, so an SOS came out to me at Pembury and as I was Midwifery Superintendent I had to provide several patients to fill the empty beds at Sevenoaks.

Julian Coxon

David and Vanessa had three children, Amanda, Timothy and Simon. They moved to Westfield near Hastings to a lovely oast house with a pool and stables for horses, near the church. Each weekend they commuted to Melton Mowbray, and David's duties included arranging hunting for Prince Charles and other members of the Royal Family, a very demanding job.

Vanessa

After David's sudden death, soon after my own husband died, Amanda married Barnabas White-Spunner and Vanessa eventually moved to Chard, to a riverside home originally part of the property belonging to the monks at Ford Abbey. Her bedroom possesses a beautiful piscina. It has been a privilege to play the organ at two family christenings in her family. Barney was given the CBE for his splendid work in Kosovo and Afghanistan, and the three children, Laetitia (Lettie), Christian (Christie) and Florence, are making progress at school while Amanda runs her two nursery schools in London.

Powderham Castle is the workplace of Tim Faulkner as he runs it for Lord Devon. Tim's wife, Charlotte, has a gift for horses and is striving to preserve the Dartmoor breed of ponies. As part of this she has produced a video in conjunction with Brian Blessed.

Victoria Storm, the elder daughter, was born after her parents had sailed to the West Indies and back. Her christening hymn was 'For those in peril on the sea'. Her sister Virginia (Ginny) is also at school locally. Tim was behind the scenes when Powderham was used to film *Remains of the Day*.

Following little Ben's tragic death, Thomas was born and I was happy to see them all, when Tim struck a boundary in the cricket match, hitting the scorer's forehead. Lord Devon was umpiring the match.

Simon (there are three Simons in the family) Faulkner is a detective in Kent. He is married to Alexandra, and they have three children, William and Suzannah, who are twins, and Theodore.

Janice Hardie (now Patterson) and her brother

Although not a member of my family, I should like to pay tribute to my God-daughter Janice Patterson, an experienced nurse, midwife and health visitor. She and her doctor husband, Don, have travelled abroad many times especially to Nepal and I feel sure their story of their medical work needs to be written.

Janice married Don in Halifax, where her father was the incumbent. I remember catching the same train home as the Manchester United team who had just lost their match. There was one other smartly dressed girl in the restaurant car, so we sat having our meal together, as I fancied myself in my large pink God-mother's hat. Much to our amusement, at every station to London, we were besieged by small boys begging for the team's autographs.

During my career I had support and friendship from many folk to whom I should pay tribute. As a raw Midwifery Superintendent, I had support from Yvonne Jordan, a very experienced midwife who knew the personalities of the 60 staff and put me right many times, even taking the Duchess of Kent round a ward when Sister sat in her office refusing to meet our Royal guest.

Dame Audrey Emerton encouraged me when beginning Nurse Auxiliary Training in the region, as did the other staff at David Salomon's House when it changed from being a convalescent home (where my mother went following a hip operation). We were responsible for training in 200 hospitals in southeast England, and valued the beautiful house, the first to have electricity in the region, and the large grounds, all the property originally of the first Jew to sit in Parliament.

Living alone after Ted's death I appreciated the friendship, especially on the phone, of Jean McBain, a fellow midwife with an ever well tuned ear, as I poured out my latest mistake or trouble. Betty Rainbow and her husband have stood by me through the years with their sincere faith and financial experience.

Christ's Hospital gives me the greatest joy, either when visiting to meet my Presentee David Smith, whom I chose out of 70 other applicants, or attending Court meetings at the Mansion House etc. The Service at St Paul's Cathedral, at which we paraded with the Lord Mayor and all the Sheriffs, led by His Highness the Duke of Gloucester, our President, was a most inspiring occasion, as was the visit of Queen Elizabeth II to Christ's Hospital in November 2003.

David Smith

Christ's Hospital

BUCKINGHAM PALACE

29th October, 2003

Dear Mrs. Coxon - Taylor,

The Queen wishes me to write and thank you for your letter following Her Majesty's visit to Christ's Hospital School on Friday, 24th October.

The Queen greatly enjoyed her visit, and much appreciated the kind message of gratitude which you have conveyed to Her Majesty, The Duke of Edinburgh and The Duke and Duchess of Gloucester.

The Queen was touched by the warmth of the welcome she received at the School, and was pleased to hear that you, too, have such happy memories of the day.

I am to thank you for the assurance of your prayers and for the good wishes and thoughtful sentiments expressed in your letter.

Yours sincerely,

Linia Henderson.

Lady-in-Waiting

Mrs. E. Coxon-Taylor

HM Queen's visit to Christ's Hospital, 2003

I remember with gratitude our old headmistress, Miss Craig, my late friends who kept up a round-robin letter for years, and music staff Miss Kemp and Miss Sinker who enabled me to get the only Gold Medal during the reign of Edward VIII for piano. Thanks to this teaching, I have been playing the organ in our Pembury village churches and at Tudeley, the church with the Chagall windows donated by the D'Avigdor Goldsmid family in memory of their daughter who drowned in a sailing accident. It was a privilege to play for Yehudi Menuhin's daughter's Godchild. The baptism of the new baby was delayed as the father, a world famous conductor, was stuck on the A21. I was terrified until after the service the baby's mother struggled up the organ stairs to thank me, and later she sent me a wonderful Japanese fan from America.

East window by Chagall in Tudeley Church,
donated in memory of Sarah D'Avigdor Goldsmid

During church services I preferred not to play psalms, but I got roped in to play at the Tunbridge Wells Crematorium, as relief organist, in 1996. All went fairly well until driving into the other cemetery chapel to play, when a *Peugeot* pick-up met me head-on at the gates. The driver was unable to read and so could not write his insurance details, but his lady friend came to his aid. I realised driving had not been a pleasure for some time and happily continued going by bus to the 'Crem' and sold my car.

A book could be written about our adventures at the Crem, and I'm always pleased to see Bert or Roy ready for me with a hot mug of tea. What a welcome after a very busy morning playing for funerals. Down in the kitchen, it is usually warm. What a variety of professions, what an interesting collection of personalities, some deeply religious but more and more services are using CD music. Recently it was Vera Lynn's, 'We'll Meet Again', and music from Andrew Lloyd Webber's *Cats* which I had never seen before. Once there was 'Land of Hope and Glory', which I painstakingly wrote out in manuscript, only to get to the chapel and find the printed copy on the organ, left by my wonderful organist friend, Cathy, with a box of delicious biscuits as a 'Thank You' for playing all day. One time all was going well until 'Guide me Oh Thou Great Jehovah', which I had carefully prepared in a lower key for the rain-drenched congregation, when half way through the address I realised the family were Welsh. Having launched into the A and M tune, I sensed a lack of audience participation. The undertaker came back to the organ as I frantically searched for Cwm Rhonda, and after a panic pause, the congregation spontaneously sang the whole hymn unaccompanied while I sat utterly mortified, covered in confusion. I had a sleepless night, returning my organist's fee next day with humble apologies.

Village school Governors suffer almost as much as staff before OFSTED Inspections, but it is a great joy to meet children in the village Post Office or *Tesco's* whom one has helped to read, and to hear that a hairdresser's brother, an uncontrollable seven-year-old previously, has a steady job and has passed his driving test.

Autumn brings cooler days but Church fetes continue, flower shows, (I got 75p for first prize in the cookery section, gooseberry fool, there were three entries!), and now the WI District Drama. In past years we had a flourishing choir which I and others enjoyed running, and most Christmas WI parties have carols after 'Jerusalem' if there is a piano in the hall.

My good friends opposite, Julie and Rob Newbould and their children Marc and Courtney, recently from Zimbabwe, collect me for church in their car. Courtney rides on Sunday morning, but my riding in the village stopped the week before my wedding, as the morning sun blinded the horse and it bolted. I decided it would not help my fiancé if I went up the aisle on a stretcher. Previously I had ridden in Scotland with a physiotherapist friend when my mother went with us, putting the car on the train to Edinburgh, and after her death, riding in the Lake District which was fine until my horse stumbled, giving me fractured ribs.

Sadly many of our former friends have dropped off the perch, but there are the frequent Ruby and Golden Wedding celebrations to enjoy and a great number of baptisms at which we, as Mother's Union members, are asked to assist.

My enjoyment of some TV programmes lately was enhanced by realising that one of the ladies in *Dad's Army* used to come round to my digs in Oxford, when I was Assistant Stage Manager, and ask for my help in learning her words as we both worked at the Oxford Playhouse.

Finally I must mention the Tudeley Music Festival run by Dr Stephen Coles, formerly a Guy's medical student who came to Pembury Hospital when I was Midwifery Superintendent. This provided hours of first class music from many brilliant musicians. He began by giving concerts in the nurses' sitting room. This Obstetric pupil, with bright pink ties, introduced us to culture many had not previously experienced. He and his wife Sarah have cared for me since my dear husband's death.

Christmas 2003 found me recovering from a usual programme of toddler's Nativity plays, several days unexpectedly filling in at the Crematorium, playing the organ for the Hospital Carol service and Over-60s Christmas Service, plus our Communion Service on December 25th in our thirteenth-century village church.

The best thing to give:
to your enemy is forgiveness;
to an opponent, tolerance;
to a friend, your heart;
to your child, a good example;
to a father, deference;
to your mother, conduct that will make her proud of you;
to yourself, respect;
to all men, charity.

(Lord Balfour)

Appendix 1

Establishing a training department –
changes, challenges, chances.

By Miss W E Coxon, SRN, SCM, MTO, Hosp Admin Cert, Senior Nursing Officer Training, Education Centre, Pembury Hospital, Tunbridge Wells, Kent.

In August 1970, it was decided to set up a nurse training department within the Tunbridge Wells and Leybourne Group of hospitals. A senior nursing officer, with responsibility for non-statutory training was appointed. The programme to be arranged included induction courses for all grades of staff, 'come back to nursing' courses, study days for trained staff, and basic courses for nursing auxiliaries. In addition, further education for all types of staff was to be promoted.

Objectives

Personal observation and experience showed a need for training. Many trained staff are lost to the profession because they lose interest in their work. This frequently occurs because senior staff do not have the time or ability to further the knowledge of trained staff, or encourage them to take further courses to widen their education. Moreover, rapid changes in medical science affect many different departments and specialties. It is important to provide all trained personnel with information regarding changes in ideas and methods; this adds interest to their work. Ward teaching must also be carried out by trained staff, using modern techniques. Above all, there must be a standardisation of teaching methods.

The objective of any training should be essentially practical: to provide increased job satisfaction and to improve recruitment. Training methods and procedures should conform to the statutory regulations of the General Nursing Council, and the Central Midwives Board.

Results

During the past three years a unifying effect has been achieved through staff from various hospitals in the Group meeting on study days. These meetings have also resulted in a noticeable improvement in morale. The training department hope that staff feel welcome and appreciated at these sessions.

During these years, at least 410 nursing auxiliaries/assistants have attended some form of training. This training may have taken the form of a three-day induction course, or a 10-week course consisting of a two-hour session once a week.

Study days for trained staff are held monthly, except in August and at Christmas. Approximately 30 to 40 staff attend on these occasions. The numbers of nursing auxiliaries/assistants who attend the four study days per year were increasing at such a rate that they had to be reduced - at the catering officer's request. The value of these lectures is that they produce improved ward work.

'Back to nursing' courses are held on three consecutive half-days in a week. Advertisements are placed in the local Press for three successive weeks and all applications receive personal attention. It is essential not to apply pressure to the trainees. Although at the end of the course some will volunteer to work immediately, many more return a few years later when their children are older. Consultants, heads of departments, and ward sisters talk about new techniques, new drugs, disposable equipment, and the senior nursing staff structure

The most popular session is in the wards, where white coats are provided; the ward sister's session is also greatly appreciated. At present, within the general division, 150 trained nurses have attended these courses over the three years, and 'Back to midwifery' courses are planned for the future.

Study days for the induction of trained staff take a morning and are held monthly. Sisters/charge nurses and staff nurses are introduced to Group methods, and a tour of the hospitals is arranged. Management aspects of the work are discussed, fire lectures are given, and during the afternoon plans are made for tutorial staff to explain clinical procedures. These sessions are most valuable for those staff trained elsewhere, especially if they have not worked in hospitals for many years.

Each month induction days are held for all grades of staff on a multidisciplinary basis. Representatives of clerical staff, laboratory technicians, students from the occupational therapy department, and others attend. Although there is a set format, lectures vary slightly according to the needs of the participants.

In-service training develops in different ways within different groups, according to past tradition, experience, and geographical layout. In addition, the future needs of the area must be considered. At present many grades are involved and it is therefore difficult to standardise methods on a national basis. Staff involved in this work have a wide variety of job descriptions, and many other responsibilities are included in their day-to-day work.

It is possible that future questionnaires on wastage and recruitment may give valuable information for research purposes. In this way it may be feasible to monitor results.

Further Education

Diploma in Nursing

This is the third year during which 10 staff have taken Part A of the Diploma on a day-release basis. While preparing for Part B examination, candidates attend a local College of Further Education for one evening a week in term-time. Consultants and others from the hospital within the Group are generous with their help and advice, both during these two-hour sessions and on the wards. This year the demand has greatly exceeded the number of vacancies available on these courses.

City and Guilds (730) Further Education Teacher's Certificate

This course is helpful to staff seconded from the group nurse training department. Nursing auxiliaries/assistants gain considerable benefit from teachers who keep up-to-date with modern methods.

Management Courses

In conjunction with tutors from the Regional Conference Centre, first line management courses (peripatetic) are arranged within the Group. Students from other areas visit the hospitals in this area as part of their course.

Records

A file of records has been compiled to give information about trained staff, the management courses they attend, previous experience and qualifications. In addition, records of nursing auxiliaries/assistants are kept; details of the courses they attend and their progress on the wards are most valuable.

Evening classes at local Colleges of Further Education

Microbiology

Ten-week courses have been held at intervals during the past three years. For two hours, once a week, trained staff attend the elementary course at their own expense (£2 per session), and in their own time. The popularity of these courses encouraged the tutor to begin an advanced course. Lectures on genetics are also planned, bearing in mind the needs of the staff in hospitals for the mentally handicapped.

Law

A short course on hospital law (five lectures for £1) is run. The lecturer is a local solicitor.

Supervisory skills

The 10-week evening course proved popular initially with the multidisciplinary staff within this Group. However, the time was changed from 7-9 pm to 4.30-6.30 pm, and this proved most impracticable for most hospital personnel. Because an increasing number of management courses are being held elsewhere, the need is not so urgent.

Study days for trained nurses

The original plan for half-day study sessions within the Group was valuable, but proved impractical for those staff who had to travel 30 to 40 miles. It has been decided, therefore, to hold study days (9 am to 4.30 pm) every month. In order that vital information can be given, ie reorganisation for 1974, ward teaching, clinical procedures, etc, the programme is repeated on three occasions.

By varying the weekdays, an opportunity is provided for all staff to attend at some time. After each study day, careful records of attendance are kept.

When the study days began, the lectures were varied and many senior staff were asked to speak. The co-operation of busy surgeons who brought slides and valuable films, and medical consultants who travelled miles to lecture, was very encouraging. No money was available to pay the speakers because the department operated on a shoestring.

However district nurses, health visitors, general practitioners, and Regional Hospital Board officers, came readily from other counties as well as our own. They participated in panel discussions and brains trusts and on subjects such as 'Home from hospital' (Dan Mason) long before 1974. The programmes were varied to suit the busy ward sister/charge nurse and included films and talks on clinical, as well as managerial, subjects.

Visits, sessions, and seminars

Nurses have to face physical weariness and mental and emotional fatigue. The need for further education should not only encourage and fit them for promotion, but also enable them to give their best for the sake of the patients. Lectures and wider experience should broaden their vision and knowledge so that they return to work, whether it be the bedside, clinic, or office, refreshed, invigorated, and with renewed inspiration.

Visits to other hospitals, coach tours to hospitals within the Group, and special study days for the individual needs of hospitals have been organised. Transport officers are helpful, and considerable use is made of cars belonging to the staff. Expenses are paid by the hospitals for official and approved journeys. Staff are sometimes asked to participate in publicity drives at local colleges and cinemas, and this provides valuable experience for those involved in in-service training.

As the training department has increased in size and commitment, other subjects have been introduced to the original job description. Special study days, such as staff appraisal sessions and seminars on the teaching of nursing assistants, require catering facilities, general preparation, and constant supervision. Other organisations, such as the local Boy Scouts and Parkinson's disease Association, enlist help from the in-service training department when running their own study days.

Lectures have been given in local schools, and slides have been collected by the local Group photographer so that photographs of hospitals throughout the Group can be shown. One series of slides depicts the progress of the patient, from the time he sees his GP, until his discharge from hospital. Another series demonstrates the work of other disciplines within the hospital: the laundry, domestic service, catering staff, etc.

Programmes for visitors from many parts of the world - mainly representatives from China, Italy, and Germany- have been enjoyed.

In preparation for an emergency, national or local, the department has been asked to arrange a training scheme for members of the local British Red Cross Society, St John Ambulance Brigade, and other voluntary organisations.

The Future

In addition to non-statutory and post-registration training, it is also essential to help with recruitment. Pre-nursing students visit the wards from local colleges. One tutor supervises them as they spend one full day a week in hospital. Projects encourage interest, and a number of students return to train within this Group.

To achieve a programme of further education, it has been essential to work in harmonious liaison with many grades of staff and many disciplines. We have been helped by our colleagues in the Education Centre and are permitted to use their equipment. This includes anatomical models, blackboards, film, slide and overhead projectors, and tape recorders. In addition, the department has access to all the libraries. In order to provide further textbooks for nursing assistants, money has been raised by bring-and-buy sales. Members of the nursing staff have been patient, and shown courtesy and understanding. Hard work and willingness to learn have earned goodwill.

Appendix 2

Establishing Nursing Auxiliary Training within the General Division

Reproduced from *Nursing Mirror,* May 31st 1974

Whatever the future envisaged by the Briggs Report, the basic question, "Who is going to nurse the patient?" remains. Who will nurse the patient when the student nurses become supernumerary? How will nursing auxiliaries be trained?

In order to satisfy a need when wards were reopened and staff were required immediately, three-day crash - or induction - courses were initiated. In addition a longer course, originally based on the National Hospital Service Reserve programme, was arranged so that staff could be trained before and after entering the wards. The three-day induction courses continue to be appreciated, and are now run at monthly intervals in the main hospitals within this Group. At the end of these days, trainees are tested and questionnaires are distributed. These are valuable when planning future sessions, as staff are refreshingly honest!

Lectures cover basic nursing procedures such as bed making, blanket baths, and lifting, as well as ethics, etiquette, and elementary anatomy and physiology. Between six and 12 nurses attend the induction course each month, and the venue varies according to the need within the Group.

The 10-week course originally began simultaneously in three general hospitals within the Division. Two-hour lectures were held on different days of the week, and the basic nursing procedures were covered in more detail than in the three-day course.

Pilot schedules have been tried whereby nursing auxiliaries have individual items initialled by their tutor and ward sisters, so that proficiency in carrying out basic nursing procedures can be demonstrated.

At the end of the 10-week course, all nursing auxiliaries who attend 70 per cent of the lectures are issued with a certificate, often greatly valued by the owner.

Months of work have been spent devising a job description, and defining nursing and non-nursing duties for nursing auxiliaries. It was clearly shown which duties may or may not be carried out. At present a similar plan to clarify the job descriptions of nursing assistants in the field of the mentally handicapped patients is being worked out.

In order to introduce these new job descriptions to the staff, the help of the nursing management was enlisted. It was feared that some staff who would be losing duties which they had carried out for many years might become frustrated and bored. The staff were anxious to quash any dissatisfaction within the ranks of student and pupil nurses, who have to obtain the necessary practical experience on the wards. Carefully prepared, it was found that nursing auxiliaries would accept changes, and yet be ready to take up the same duties again if students were not on the ward.

Annual Competition

A competition, initiated last year, encouraged practical training and boosted morale. Teams of four nursing auxiliaries/assistants competed for a shield. The competition was adjudicated in the practical classroom of the education centre. A panel of judges, representing the various Divisions within the Group, gave each team 10 minutes to perform simple duties for three 'real patients'. These included bed making, lifting, and bandaging. Marks were carefully allocated, and the smallest hospital within the Group won the shield (largely due to their teamwork).

This year the competition will be held in a hospital for the mentally handicapped.

Follow-up

Wherever possible, it is essential to contact staff at their place of work after they have completed a course. Sisters/charge nurses within the Group nurse training department aim to work on the wards with nursing auxiliaries/assistants. It is often valuable to visit new staff to iron out difficulties which may have occurred such as problems with uniform or pay. At present, one sister or charge nurse within the department is responsible for in-service training for each large hospital and some smaller ones.

Role of the Nursing Officer

Nursing officers attached to the department have an administrative or an advisory role. They contribute ideas, and take part in clinical and theoretical' teaching with a surprising amount of energy, enthusiasm, and enterprise. During the past three years a nursing officer with many years' experience has run courses for nursing assistants within two hospitals containing 1,600 patients. Soon after his appointment, he was joined by a ward sister, also very experienced, who undertook the practical teaching in the clinical situation.

Induction Course

The highly specialised course of 30 lectures was developed successfully, but experience proved that a shorter course of 12 two-hour talks maintained greater interest. Both the nursing assistants taking the course, and their ward sisters/charge nurses who had to run the wards during their absence, appeared to benefit from a shorter course which included practical tuition. Another nursing officer with considerable teaching experience has now joined the team. She is responsible for training cadets within that hospital, and her appointment has enabled a full programme of induction courses and multi- disciplinary lectures to be given. Recruitment and the publication of the hospital magazine are also included in the activities of the nursing officers.

It was found that, in addition to group study days, it was necessary to organise special lectures relevant to the needs of those working in hospitals for the mentally subnormal. SEN refresher courses were valuable, especially for those who had gained State Enrolled status through experience. Lectures have been given during the night by staff attached to the department, and nursing auxiliaries/assistants who attend study days are paid if they normally work on night duty.

Departmental Routine

Over three years staff within the Group nurse training department has increased by 700 per cent. At first all communications were written by hand and it was important to establish methods and routes by which to send information on a two-way basis. The most successful method of spreading news was by word of mouth and by foot. The use of cars was the next best way, followed by the hospital internal postal system, in the Group van driver. At the beginning busy secretaries and friends offered help. We discovered which notice boards were used and read, and also how the grapevine functioned, ie where the right word in the right place did the most good. We also learnt who were the sisters who passed on messages to their staff and who were not.

Obtaining information from individuals is always difficult unless letters enclose self-addressed envelopes. The catering officers in all hospitals have been models of helpfulness and co- operation, but nobody likes to plan lunch for 40 nursing auxiliaries/assistants, only to find the day before that 60 are coming, and on the day, see 80 appear.

A nursing officer must be absolutely sincere. She must be able to see the problems and know some of the answers. She must have an understanding and sympathy for all grades of staff. In the position of a mature watchdog or ombudsman, the nurse training officer must not lose integrity and must be discreet throughout all the changes of Salmon, the reorganisation of the NHS, and Briggs. There must be no fear of speaking out when necessary.

Although the department operates on a shoestring, it has been helped by the use of classrooms (practical and theoretical) and equipment in the education centre. Few areas have the opportunity afforded to this Group, of using initiative and of obtaining the help of such a wide grade of staff in so many disciplines.

The work has produced changes; it has given the staff challenges, but on all occasions chances have been given to everybody associated with the department.

Acknowledgments

The department would like to express its gratitude to many who have helped to establish these new schemes. It is sensitive to the rising and falling temperatures within a Group undergoing change.

I should like to thank Miss A C Emerton, Chief Nursing Officer, for her help in establishing this department, and her continued support. Also Mrs M P Crawford, Principal Nursing Officer, Education, for allowing us to hold many of our courses in the Education Centre, Pembury Hospital.

As the group barometer fluctuates, our training methods aim to keep a steady balance and maintain clear perspective in these days of changes, challenges and chances.

Presentation of shield to winning team of the Nursing Assistants/ Auxiliaries' Competition 1973.

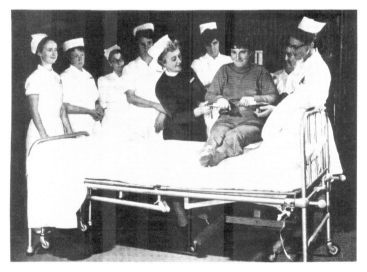

A demonstration by Mrs Yvonne Kennard to nursing auxiliaries
Photograph by courtesy of P Broadbury, Queen Victoria Hospital.

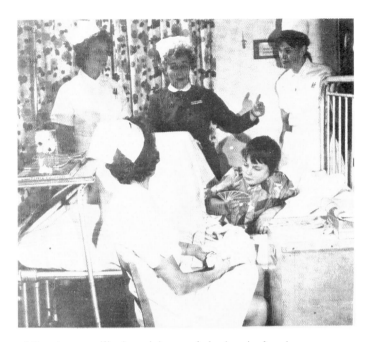

Nursing auxiliaries visit ward during induction course
Photograph by courtesy of P Bradbury, Queen Victoria Hospital
Photographs courtesy of the *Kent and Sussex Courier,*
Tunbridge Wells Advertiser and *The Nursing Mirror*

Appendix 3

The Advance of Medicine in a Kent Village

Reproduced from *Nurse and Health Visitor Journal*, May 1970

By Miss W Elizabeth Coxon, SRN, SCM, MTD, Hosp Admin Cert, midwifery superintendent, Pembury Hospital.

The author outlines the history of Pembury Hospital in Kent from 1837 to March 1969 when a new labour ward suite was opened by Her Royal Highness, the Duchess of Kent

Exchange an air-raid shelter from World War II for a light, well planned labour ward suite. Build on land where last year wild orchids were picked. Site a brand new milk kitchen-progress!

The first recorded birth in the workhouse, known as the Tonbridge Union in the village of Pembury, was on December 15th, 1835. This building was enlarged in 1887 for the treatment of infectious diseases and became a hospital "to accommodate sixteen patients, with two wards, a caretaker's cottage and a walled garden for the patients' use." But the village of 'Pepenbury' is much older than its nearby neighbour, Tunbridge Wells. Called in Textus Roffensis Pepingberia, then later Pepenbery-pronounced Pembury, we see that Turner's etching is clearly marked Pembury.

History of the Village

At the time of Caesar's invasion of Britain in 55 B.C., the inhabitants of Kent were "clothed in the skins of wild beasts. The hair of their heads they wore long, but shaved all the face except the upper lip. They were tall in their persons and remarkably honest and ingenuous. In general they lived to a great age probably owing to their exercise, sobriety and temperance, as well as the wholesomeness of the climate."

As years went by Pope Gregory IX in 1239 granted a licence to the Abbot and Convent of Begham (now known as Bayham) to 'hold Pembury Church'. The manors of Pepenbury Magna and Parva were also given to the Abbey until the dissolution of the monasteries under Henry VIII. They were then surrendered to Cardinal Wolsey.

Lengthy tales of the noble ownership of the village property are recorded in Hasted's *History of Kent*. In 1702 almshouses were bequeathed to the village. In 1798 it is recorded that "A fair is held in this parish on Whit Tuesday for cattle, toys and pedlary."

Meanwhile changes in England had affected the simple villagers. In 1555 it is recorded in Fox's *Book of Martyrs*, that "Margery Polley, widow, sometime wife of Richard Polley of Pepingbery, was accused and brought before the Bishop of Rochester." He "rose to dash the silly poor woman," and demanded "a true full and plain answer to the articles against her." She was condemned at the beginning of June and burnt at the stake in July – the first woman martyr in England.

Founding of the Hospital

Changing opinion and a sense of responsibility became more widespread; and so by order of the Poor Law Commissioners there was held, on November 7th 1835, the first meeting of the Guardians of the Tonbridge Union. (Tunbryege = Anglo Saxon Town of Bridges – although badly submerged during the 1968 floods). At this initial meeting £252 was the sum fixed to be paid for the patients' medical care with ten shillings for each maternity case.

Wandering bands of tramps continued to move from workhouse to workhouse. Records were kept of these 'Casuals'. The day and hour of each admission were recorded, together with their age, number of children and calling or occupation.

The work carried out in the Union was noted e.g., stone breaking, working in the garden or making mail bags – some records show "Reason for not working – Frosty." The cells used for stone breaking can still be seen in part of the hospital today. Former inmates had to break a certain quantity of stone and pass it through a fine grill before they were allowed to move on. Some wayfarers were referred to the medical officers, others handed to the police, but all were given food and lodging. Parish relief was available and meanwhile the hospital and Union developed side by side.

An agreement for nurses' training was drawn up in 1924 and application made for Pembury to be recognised as a minor training school for nurses, "and in the case of such nurses found to be suitable, midwifery training for the purpose of qualifying for the certificate of the Central Midwives Board."

The Superintendent Nurses' Reports during that decade were enlightening. In 1925 it was mentioned that "Extra soft pillows are urgently required for the patients. The present stock of 134 does not allow one for each patient. I would like the uniform for probationers to be made on the premises. At present they are getting £6 in lieu thereof. I find they do not always spend the money on uniform and in consequence are untidy when on duty. I would suggest that one sister be appointed permanently to the post of Night Sister at the salary of £75 8s. 0d. per annum as I find Ward Sisters reluctant to do night duty."

The report goes on: "We suffer from mice which burrow right into the loaves-something should be done as it is most unhealthy for people to eat bread which has been run over by mice." However, "the patients speak very highly of the care they are receiving and the new arrangement is exceedingly satisfactory." The minutes of the Management Committee then report, next to an advertisement for probationer nurses that the hospital is buying and selling pigs.

Villagers' 'Do it Yourself' Medicine

Local inhabitants of the village today tell of prescriptions used in their life-time, for sickness at home: "Ivy leaves for chilblains, ripe acorns for diarrhoea, yellow barbary bark for bilious attacks and boiled onions tied to the ear for earache. A special pan was kept for frying the heads of adders, as the oil obtained therefrom was applied with a feather to cure snake bites."

Spectacles were sold at the door by a high-hated, black coated, white bearded gentleman who sold each pair for 3s 6d. Teeth, before the First World War, were sold at 'cut-price' by an American gentleman (to the dismay of local dentists). He charged 30s per set, extractions free. No ambulance was available but on one occasion an injured man was conveyed to hospital on a shed door in a chimney sweep's cart.

The occupations of the patients were often similar to those of our patients today, basket makers, tree fellers, saddle makers, cricket ball makers, fruit and hop pickers. Now, however, the husbands are often commuters, garage attendants or long distance drivers – the changing face of Britain.

World Wars I and II

During the first World War a VAD hospital was set up in the Church Institute. World War II however, brought the whole of the training section of Guy's Hospital into the village. Much has been written of this notable period in the hospital's history. Famous names in both the medical and nursing professions were connected with the work that was brilliantly carried out at Pembury.

One amusing fact was that a trainee nurse was amazed to find under her mattress, in the room to which she was evacuated in 1939, a pair of tramp's trousers neatly laid and pressed.

As the war drew to its close the Guy's staff returned to London. It is said that the last flying bomb (the dreaded 'doodle bug') actually fell in Pembury village. Staff gave up digging their potatoes for night duty supper, a duty some present staff remember well, and the work of the hospital carried on.

A New Maternity Wing Envisaged and Built

The maternity workload was now increasing, and because of a recent increase in London commuters, the rapidly expanding neighbourhood necessitated an enlarged hospital midwifery service. Hospital staff were invited to carry out research on the problems. Doctors and midwives then recorded their views and submitted plans. Meetings were held with administrators, architects and engineers, with medical officials and senior nurses all contributing ideas. Eventually a decision on the site and design was reached, lists of equipment were drawn up, operational policies discussed and the work finally started in January 1968.

Snowy blizzards and local floods took their toll of building days. At last, on one cold February day this year, the first patients were admitted for delivery. Now pupil midwives (Part I and II), obstetric nurses and medical students can witness deliveries as part of their training in a splendid new labour ward suite.

Based on the race-track design, there are three multipurpose rooms and two first stage rooms all with an excellent call system, and also a large delivery room and a theatre for Caesarean sections. A useful duty room for nurses is centrally placed. Here there is a blackboard for teaching purposes and a 'peg-board' to display the pupils' records of progress during training. A convenient small kitchen is nearby to provide drinks and a light diet, if it is permitted, for the patients in labour. One interesting innovation is a floating rubber bell push which enables a patient to summon help while in her bath.

Throughout the unit there is a sense of colour, gay paint, chequered floors, delightful curtains, carpets and furniture. All create a bright and light atmosphere. The new much needed milk kitchen is nearby and has facilities to supply the whole maternity unit with daily feeds. A deep pass-through sink with a large refrigerator are well sited. Firms whose names are household words have contributed generously towards the cost of some of this equipment.

And so, on a cold March day last year, the maternity unit at Pembury was honoured by a Royal Visitor.

The babies born in 1969 are indeed fortunate. Their mothers can look over the Weald of Kent to the green downs beyond blossom-filled valleys whilst listening to the cuckoo. They can also remember that their new labour ward suite was opened by no less a person than that gracious lady, Her Royal Highness the Duchess of Kent.

Acknowledgement

I wish to thank the Trustees of the British Museum, also the County Archivist and Kent County Council for permission to carry out research on their premises.

Mill, Kent (reproduced by courtesy of The Trustees. British Museum)

Burning at the stake in Pembury of Margery Polley, the first woman martyr in England – from Fox's Book of Martyrs.

193

Appendix 4

Report of Scholarship Tour April 1ˢᵗ – July 3ʳᵈ 1964 Netherlands - North Germany – Sweden - Finland – South Germany - Switzerland – France

Thanks to the excellent organisation of the Royal College of Midwives and the Royal College of Nursing, I was enabled to visit several hospitals in Britain before leaving on my tour. This proved a most helpful and fruitful experience.

In June 1963 I also spent two weeks in Spain with 2,000 midwives at the International Congress in Madrid and then in South Spain, where I visited a large hospital. The number of patients with tuberculosis and with gross deformities was frightening in 1964 in Europe.

During September I visited the Simpson Memorial Maternity Pavilion, the Royal Infirmary, Edinburgh and also the University Nursing Studies Unit in that city. Newcastle on Tyne was the next stop where I visited the Ante-Natal and Baby Clinics and also saw patients in their own homes. The domiciliary work was particularly well organised.

The Bradford 48-hour discharge scheme interested me from the Maternity angle, and the Birmingham Maternity and Sorrento Hospitals were most instructive. Cardiff and Southampton proved stimulating, as the Maternity Hospitals are linked with the Universities.

This year I paid visits to University College Hospital, Saint Bartholomew's Hospital and the Middlesex Hospital and this period was a fitting climax to my preparations.

HOLLAND April 1ˢᵗ

The sight of the early bulb-fields in bloom is unforgettable. Visits to the Polders - reclaimed land which was formerly the sea bed, strike one afresh, that man has at his disposal the amazing capacity for feeding millions of the world population.

The School of Midwives at Amsterdam is an old hospital with somewhat conservative though sound methods. Good relaxation classes were demonstrated but there was a need for new ideas to implement the basic care. I was struck by poor accommodation for the nurses, conditions which were similar to those that I had seen in Spain.

The School of Midwives at Heerlen was, by contrast, a new hospital run under Roman Catholic orders, with some lay staff as well as the Sisters. Here I was pleased to meet one of my ex-pupil midwives who showed me much of the excellent new equipment in the Labour Ward and Theatre. I was particularly interested in the Children's Department though one tragic case was a two year old hydrocephalic child with a head circumference of 36 centimetres - cared for devotedly by the Sisters. There were dozens of beautiful babies, of unmarried mothers. Both mothers and their infants stayed in hospital for many months if necessary.

The pupil midwives' training was sound, and fitted them admirably for their hospital and domiciliary future. The lectures I attended (in Dutch) were of interest, and I was shown all over the laundry, kitchen and other parts of the hospital, enabling me to make copious notes on equipment and training methods.

The training of a midwife took two years (if they were fully trained nurses); 40% of the deliveries took place in hospital, 60% at home. Approximately 934 midwives were practising when I visited Holland - the population was 11 million. There were no pensions organised for the midwives. The cost of a delivery by a midwife was 80 Gulder (£7) so that in order to make a living it might be necessary to take 120 deliveries a year. This was a real problem, as the doctors charged 200 Guilder (£17. 10. 0.) and as a 'status symbol' a doctor's delivery was much sought after. There was rivalry between the professions and in some cases financial hardship for the midwife.

One 70 year old midwife delivered 140 babies last year (riding a bicycle on her visits).

The Green Cross Organisation is a National Association responsible for much domiciliary work. Other religious organisations are the Yellow Green Cross and Orange Green Cross which care for patients outside hospital. At Hendrik Ido Ambacht I stayed with the delightful family of the District Midwife and observed the delivery of a healthy baby. No sedation was given to the mother, and a maternity aide did most of the manual work of cleaning, bathing the baby etc. Visits to post-natal patients were interesting, as I noted everywhere extreme cleanliness, such as I also saw in the Finnish homes.

NORTH GERMANY - HAMBURG

Frauenklinik und Hebammenlehranstall - FINKENAU

1914 - 753 deliveries. 1963 – 5,416 deliveries.

A most interesting ten days, spent mostly in the Labour Ward. Pupil Midwives trained for one-and-a-half years - but if not qualified, two years. Most deliveries were carried out in hospital.

The pupils obtained about 250 deliveries in two years and learned how to suture the perineum. I found the pace very great, and, although technically as good as possible, personal care of the patients was obviously neglected. I was allowed to deliver a Scots girl from Aberdeen. Other cases I witnessed included a badly asphyxiated baby and a severe pre-eclamptic patient.

New work:

Amnioscopy was carried out. This procedure was to enable the surgeon to decide if the patient has a post-mature baby.

The Malmstrom Vacuum Extractor was used.

Research was being carried out in anaesthetics and Dr Wendl had some interesting new equipment for baby resuscitation. Drugs were used greatly, especially 'the Cocktail' – Dolantin, Megaphen and Atonil; this I found effective at the end of the first stage of labour. Forceps deliveries and Caesarean Sections were witnessed whilst I worked there, and blood was cross-matched in the labour ward by doctors when necessary but practically no ante-natal care was carried out. The Milk Kitchen was of interest in this and other countries. Expressed breast milk was collected from the city and the midwife paid for obtaining it. The milk, when sterilised, was sent over 500 kilometres in wooden boxes to other hospitals, as needed, by train. The patients were paid four marks per litre. The milk was tested for fat and protein content. The ultraviolet lamp indicated if the milk was breast milk or cow's milk.

St George's Hospital, Hamburg

A fascinating hospital, old yet with a magnificent new suite of operating theatres. (The scrub basins produced water, as the hand entered the basin - no taps - no foot pedals.)

The new Nurses' Home was being built with a wonderful view over the Alter.

Kinderkrankenhause, Borgfelde

Excellent technique in the Nursery, Isolettes were used and the Children's Occupational Therapy department was most interesting. Mosaics were made by the children themselves for the front hall of the hospital. A plastic bag was invented by a nurse for suspending a baby during X-ray treatment. More encouragement should be given to our nurses to use such initiative.

The Hellman Private Maternity Clinic was visited. Here the Grantley Dick Read technique was practised. Frau Springborn, the present President of the International Confederation of Midwives, was visiting Hamburg and I was privileged to meet her and able to discuss the forthcoming Congress in Berlin in 1966. It has been a pleasure to meet her again in London this September.

Administration of Midwifery

This was largely in the hands of the consultants which resulted in a lack of initiative on the part of the midwives. Many laborious duties were still carried out, the making of dressings, sterilisation of equipment and domestic duties.

Refresher courses were organised for all midwives in Hamburg at present. Patients remained in hospital for about eight days unless there was a bed shortage. Every city was paid at a different rate and midwives tended to work in areas where the salaries were the highest.

During my visit to Hamburg I was able to visit the new Opera House to see Puccini's *Madam Butterfly*, visit the magnificent Planten den Blumen, St Michael's Church - the famous Rathaus and the chief museum. One day I took a boat trip to Blankenese on the Elbe and attended an unforgettable Bach Abend in one of the churches rebuilt after the war.

SWEDEN

Flying via Copenhagen I arrived in Gotenburg and was joined by two other Scottish Midwife Scholars.

The Midwifery School at Gotenburg

The equipment was good but already new buildings were planned in the near future. The nurses' uniforms were particularly attractive.

The Midwifery training lasted 18 months - this is a shorter period than previously but during this time they obtain wide experience. They were taught advanced techniques such as saturating episiotomies and applying Malmstrom's Extractor themselves.

Unfortunately Professor Malmstrom was ill, so we were unable to meet him, but his deputy, Professor Bergman, was most kind and helpful. In every training school I was given sheaves of typed programmes of training schemes and ward charts in English and the language of the country.

We moved to Stockholm and had the great pleasure of meeting Miss Erup – the President of the Midwives' Association in Scandinavia. Her hospitality was boundless and she spent a whole morning telling us of the Swedish Midwifery history and plans for the future. An interesting point, stressed, was that the pupil midwives do not take their examinations until they are ready to do so, and therefore all pass successfully.

Unfortunately our Swedish professional programme was so full that there was not time to visit the factories and attend a course of Industrial Nursing which was in progress at the time we visited Stockholm.

Karolinska Hospital, Stockholm

Our visit to this great hospital provided interest, as research into toxaemia was being carried out. Although not so modern as some other hospitals we visited, we watched deliveries and had interesting discussions with the doctors in this hospital and then rushed off in time to see the arrival of the King and Queen of the Belgians on a State Visit to Stockholm.

One evening I attended the opera - to see Falstaff (Verdi) and was able to see the 'Vana' ship submerged for so many years in the harbour. The wonderful Town Hall, the zoo at Skanson and other sights were unforgettable. Stockholm is surely well named the Venice of the North.

A distressing fact about Swedish Hospitals was that some had to close in the summer when staff had holidays. There was a great shortage of nurses.

Södersjukhuset

An impersonal great hospital, it was built in 1943 with underground theatres and wards many metres deep - in case of war emergency; a railway was connected, but the whole plan never required. The usual Swedish custom of using scooters in the hospital corridors was noted. I was impressed by the psychiatric unit and the intensive care unit, to the latter one or two attempted suicides are admitted daily. The legal abortion rule needs revision by Parliament.

Opposite our flat we were happy to observe the drunken antics of the inmates of a large Alcoholic Institution.

The Midwives School in this hospital was well planned. The nurses' sitting rooms and canteens were large and splendidly designed and equipped. The classrooms were richly supplied with visual aids and a magnificent selection of models and specimens.

On the Ascension Day holiday we were invited to the Nurses Cottage where we picnicked off home cooked food by the seaside and chopped and sawed quantities of wood (the quantity chopped by British Midwives was rather less than more!).

Almanna Barnbordshuset

Here we saw Relaxation Classes under Mrs Ringdahl to music of her own choice. Records were sold so that mothers could practise exercises and relaxation at home. Taped recordings were made in various languages so that labouring mothers could listen to relaxation and breathing advice in their mother tongue.

Södersjukhuset, Stockholm

Södersjukhuset Chapel

Our visit to Uppsala Hospital was of interest, for we learnt of Professor Gernzell's work and research, particularly with regard to the modified pregnancy hormone test. The huge hospital would have provided interest for hours but there was time for little except witnessing a delivery and a brief tour of the Maternity Department. During the morning we had been taken by the midwives on their off duty day, many kilometres to ENKOPING. This hospital, though small, is one of the most modern in Sweden.

On another day we paid a visit to Parliament organised by a Member of Parliament who fights much for the midwives in Sweden, Miss Astrid Kristianson.

It was a shock to observe the rising statistics of Venereal Diseases and also the increase in illegitimacy. I was however glad to learn of a petition by 140 doctors to the King of Sweden concerning this matter. This document stated a need for character training in the youth of the country and is worthy of study in our country too. It has sound facts and concrete positive ideas on these subjects.

A petition to the King had been made, too, for a third Midwifery School in Sweden. Regular refresher courses were already organised.

FINLAND

This was in some respects my happiest visit. We stayed in the flat of the Midwives Association and everywhere received great kindness.

The visit to the Board of Health with the chief Midwife and also the Helsinki City Health Service gave us much food for thought. The domiciliary work was of the greatest interest to me. Ante-natal and Infant Welfare Clinics were visited, and I observed well organised Relaxation Classes and efficient care of post-natal patients. The maternity pack supplied free to all mothers was particularly impressive and contained the following items:

Eiderdown, blanket, sheets, flannelette blanket, wool for knitting, enamel basin, large bar of washing soap, pins, soap for mother and baby, maternity pads, hair brush and cream for baby, plastic mackintosh, paper towel, plastic mattress, fine muslin napkins, bonnet, 4 pairs of knickers for baby, 4 jackets and vests, paper sheet, frill and lace (typical of Finnish baby's costume). All are supplied in a large cardboard container which is big enough to be a cot for the first few weeks. The whole can be claimed after 6 months of pregnancy.

The domiciliary bags were of interest, but like the Swedish bags, contained much heavy equipment which we would consider cumbersome and unnecessary. However distances are so great and helicopters, although widely used, did not reach all areas the midwife must visit.

Our visit to the most modern cancer hospital in Europe was peaceful and impressive. The equipment was excellent, some having been given by a past President of Finland.

During the Whitsun week-end I attended the village church where I met the Head of the Commune. A most moving memorial service was held for those who fell in the war (one in seven women were widows after the war).

A visit to the Health House at Mantsala was most inspiring especially when refreshed with a sauna and a day out in the country watching Finnish dancing and listening to the fascinating folk tunes.

The next day we visited the home for cripples where boys and girls of all ages were taught crafts - wood and metalwork etc, care of pigs, sheep and cows, horticulture and agriculture. Originally the buildings were for people injured during the war but they had been extended to care for all types of crippled people. The farm was well run, and we visited the cattle and saw the work shops and gardens.

During this week too, I visited Parliament and spent an interesting evening with a friend who in an MP. She was fighting for nurses' rights and for the maintenance of right standards of behaviour and character in youth today.

Helsinki Midwives Training School
(note public transport to the door)

A visit to the Maternity School in Helsinki was a joy, as the architecture and equipment were among the most modern I had seen. The race track scheme of wards, the beautiful classrooms, the chance to meet English-speaking midwives who had trained in England and knew many mutual friends, added to the interest.

As above – note five blocks for senior medical
and nursing staff in residence

It was not possible to visit Lapland as the snows were melting and journeys overland from the airport were not advisable, so we were spared being attacked by mosquitoes. We heard much of the health problems. Rickets was prevalent due to lack of daylight. Transport was still a problem (though helicopters were used greatly for maternity cases).

During this visit I met another scholar (an Egyptian Lady Doctor) sent by the World Health Organisation. She came with us, although tired after a long tour, and told us of the health services in her country today. We invited her to join us to listen to the University performance of Handel's *Messiah* and she asked us many questions about Christianity.

The Mannerheim War Memorial was of real interest as was the Orthodox Church and a concert given by Sibelius Academy students in an extremely modern church. The market was fascinating, and I spent a considerable time exploring the city.

Koskela Hospital for geriatric patients was well run, well equipped with a very happy atmosphere.

This hospital was also full of interest. Particularly I noted the psychiatric children, children from difficult homes and 'Key children' and heard encouraging stories of how they were cared for and regained powers of hearing and speech, formerly unused in cases where they were rejected by their families.

We spent three days in Turku where Miss Heide Soila arranged a fascinating programme in her hospital and the beauty spots of the city and University. We were privileged to see over the largest factory in Finland producing electricity at Naantali, and spent a wonderful evening with the director and his family. We met by chance in Turku a Japanese boy, deaf and dumb, who was being taken across Europe by a philanthropic American in the hope of obtaining treatment for the boy.

SOUTH GERMANY

Heidelberg

I was privileged to attend several University lectures given to medical and nursing students. These were generally of a high standard; but I was amazed at the behaviour of the students, and there appeared an extraordinary lack of sterility in the operating theatre. This was being changed under the new Professorship. One extremely serious case of ruptured uterus occurred whilst I was there, the patient receiving about 30 pints of intravenous fluid of various types.

The babies were very well cared for. During my stay one professor's wife produced healthy triplets, to the great joy of his students. When he returned to his lecture he apologised for his lateness saying, "Forgive me, gentlemen, it is not every day one becomes a father of triplets," – loud applause by high-spirited students. (The babies were 0 Rh+, A Rh+ and 0 Rh- Blood Group.)

The Varicose Vein Clinic was of interest, and emphasised the increase in average weight of many German women following the war. Thus diseases of the Affluent Society were another problem. Diabetes was notably on the increase too. As one doctor said, "Women take slimming pills like bon-bons." Another sad point is that 1,400 died on the Autobahns last year.

Alcoholism was also a grave problem, as in Sweden.

The University Children's Clinic

This had a remarkable occupational therapy department. A sister who had been ill and unable to work on the ward was encouraged to learn craft in order to teach student nurses. In preparation for children's care, this was remarkably successful.

A friend of my family was a Consultant Paediatrician in the city and he felt that 50% of the children he treated had illnesses psychosomatic in origin, due to unhappy homes.

The morning spent with the Heidelberg District Public Health Doctor was instructive, but revealed a lack of Public Health facilities. There was little or no ante-natal care and no supervision of mothers when they returned home from hospital.

One of the problems was the care of the displaced older people from the East Zone. I learnt that at least ten young people a day escaped from behind the Iron Curtain.

The most interesting but saddest visit was to the deformed babies due to the drug Thalidomide, at Schlierbach; and we had a wonderful opportunity seeing the splendid work that is being achieved there.

The Heidelberg Maternity Unit included in the pupil midwives' training regular lectures by the Priests of two denominations. Some points were discussed such as Baptism, Extreme Unction, Sterilisation and Sexual Hygiene, and the lectures appeared to play a valuable part in the public training. I was interested in the Insurance Scheme for patients and hospital statistics. The Heart-Lung machine was shown to me in great detail and I found the University atmosphere most stimulating.

In retrospect, I felt that some of the nurses in Germany were unwilling to face the full responsibility for their nation - as was the case in Britain.

The leaders of the new Nursing Schools were however training abroad. The older schemes of Red Cross training were, although technically excellent, not adequate for contemporary youth and recruits were short. One midwife whom I met had her own nursing home and had had no holiday since 1937.

I cannot end a report on Heidelberg without mentioning the wonderful social plans that were made for me. The evening at the Opera to see *Don Pasquale*, the unforgettable concert at the castle in the open air. Mozart's flute music accompanied by the sound of pigeons flying home to roost in the floodlit Renaissance building, the exciting International boat race on the Necker, the magnificent firework display, were all inspiring.

A visit to the world-famous library to see irreplaceable manuscripts and books from every country and a visit to the famous Students' Prison were full of additional interest and education.

From the professional angle, the nurses training was gradually acquiring new ideas, the pupils paid for their tuition and were supernumerary when first working on the wards. This allowed them to observe without having responsibility for the patients. I felt this was a satisfactory method but would be impossible with our current health service in Britain – though the Platt report might help to remedy this.

Flying to Lausanne, I had a few hours in Frankfurt to visit the city, especially Goethe's house. The flight to Geneva was magnificent, with clear views of the mountains.

SWITZERLAND

Lausanne Hopital Cantonal

Although the Midwifery training was studied in detail, I observed many other interesting points.

The Curie Ward

Here large quantities of radium were used in the department with full precautions and protection for the staff.

I attended several meetings of the General and Maternity Staff in the hospital. Administration was discussed with Matron and I had interesting talks with the tutors on training schemes. One interesting visit was to the Blood Donor's department.

La Source – the oldest existing Nurses training establishment - impressed me with the modern ideas of the matron, who trained in America, as did the head of the 'Nurses' School in Heidelburg.

Domiciliary Nursing is organised by the Red Cross but owing to shortage of time it was not possible to observe this first-hand.

211

Two visits to *Nestlé's* factories were arranged. The first enabled us to watch chocolate and *Nescafe* being made. We discussed with the factory's nurse her work and her touch with the factory's many workers of different nationalities. At Vevey our programme included a fascinating view of the *Nestlé's* Pouponniére given to the town for the care of unfortunate babies of unmarried mothers. They were put out in the sun in enchanting pink-frilled prams. Our morning concluded with luncheon by the lake of freshly caught fish. We saw the production of many *Nestlé's* baby foods Nido, Nesco, Nestrovit, Nidex, Arobon, etc, observing the roller-dried milk and many other points of interest.

Returning to the hospital in Lausanne, I visited the gynaecological unit staffed by nursing teams. The tutors were active, teaching clinically in the wards. The professor had much administrative power and arranges Refresher Courses for the Midwifery Staff. I heard of the interesting Home Help System. The labour problem is acute today in Switzerland. Domestic help was difficult, and carried out largely by foreigners, as was most of the manual work in Switzerland.

Geneva Hospital Cantonal

Here staff meetings at all grades were held weekly and staff shortage were apparent, even in departments with magnificent new buildings. Staying a week at the children's clinic nearby, I saw the most advanced Milk Kitchen of my tours. The whole clinic was modern with splendid isolation cubicles for the infants.

The new buildings of the general hospital had much new equipment, including beds which lift and turn at the touch of an electric button, and I was able to photograph points of interest.

World Health Organisation

Here I was given an opportunity to visit Maria Tito do Moraes and Miss Creelman in order to discuss with them the many aspects of midwifery and general medical problems.

Owing to the *Air France* strike, we had an enforced train journey, which proved comfortable and interesting, as we had intelligent companions from several countries in our carriage, and seven hours instead of one to discuss world affairs during our time together.

FRANCE July 25ᵗʰ

Paris Lamaze Centre de Sante des Metallurgistes

Here I listened to a full course of lectures on 'Accouchement sans douleur' given by midwives and doctors. These lasted approximately 14 hours and were attended by pregnant mothers and their husbands. Only one breech delivery was witnessed during the whole week - the other cases we were told, were not suitable for witness cases.

St Denis Hospital

This was built in 1960 by the same Syndicate of Metallurgistes, in a rapidly expanding area of Paris. The equipment was good in idea, but usually of inferior materials. The staff uniform was strangely un-professional by British standards. The same method of preparation was given to the mothers as in the previous hospital and good work appeared to be carried out.

Hotel de Dieu

This hospital was visited, but with difficulty. It was a sore disappointment, considering the connection with Florence Nightingale. The old wards in attics, the wooden stairs which she may have herself trodden and the indifferent attitude of the staff would have distressed her. There was little to recommend nursing in France; yet there was a great underlying passion for justice, freedom and equality which should be mobilised to produce fine work in nursing fields.

In conclusion, the main impression made upon me by this extensive and varied tour, was that much excellent work was being performed and a great deal of experimental study carried out. There was, however in many cases, an apparent lank of overall responsibility in all grades of the Nursing Profession for the condition of the world around them.

Many of our patients which required nursing care should not have been in hospital. These included many types of mentally disturbed folk, attempted suicides, women having illegitimate children, criminal abortion, or venereal diseases. Such patients were ill through wrong relationships, personality problems and lack of specific purpose in life. Their small aims allowed selfish indulgences, bitterness and impurity in their way of living. (Now in 2004 there are great problems with alcoholism, drugs and AIDS).

By the end of my tour I felt that we had once more reached a stage in the life of our nations when the nurse needed to re-evaluate her position and responsibility in society. Her rank rightly understood, is the equal of that, and indeed greater than that, of any Cabinet Minister.

It seemed to me that the modern hospital must do more than send people back with new health. It must return them to the community with new aims and standards. Health is more than a state of feeling well in mind, body and spirit. It is a means to a richer life of service.

As midwives I felt we could help mothers to build sound homes and give character training to their families. The true destiny of women was to inspire those around us to accept responsibility. The building of character must once again become the aim for the upbringing of the next generations, and we must get leaders who will stand for what is right whatever the cost.

Through the coming years I shall remember with gratitude this three months tour given in memory of those who worked in the Nursing Profession, sacrificed and died during the war.

Appendix 5

Management Development Workshop I
Reproduced from *Nursing Focus*, 1981

ELIZABETH COXON TAYLOR, Senior Training Officer, Nursing, South East Thames Regional Health Authority.

The aim of management role development workshops was to bring together managers carrying out the same functions at the same level, in order to agree priorities in their job *. They were to identify improvement opportunities and to find ways in which their work could be carried out making the best use of available resources. When nursing officer workshops began in the South East Thames Regional Health Authority, the author ran them for nursing officers and over a period of two years nearly 700 officers attended.

A manager's true worth to his company may sometimes be measured by the time he could remain dead in his office without anybody noticing it. (1)

Whereas this is not a policy to be recommended in the National Health Service, an interesting and valuable exercise has been carried out in the South East Thames Region. A series of two-day workshops was run to obtain maximum return from training in a cost-effective manner. The purpose of the workshop was explained to nursing officers and reference made to *The Grey Book* (2), *The Priorities for Health and Social Services Consultative Document* (3) and *Sharing Resources for Health in England* (4). Surprisingly few nurses had read these documents. The course members then studied a chart which showed the different ways in which each saw his or her own job, the job of the person above, and the job of the colleague below.

The First Day

As we welcomed course members with coffee, they were asked to say why they had come! There was much laughter as with a chorus-like chant one by one repeated "I was sent." In reality the degree of involvement by immediate superiors in improved pre-course selection, preparation and follow-up, reveals a contradictory picture (5). People relaxed as the day went on and began to make new friends across the tables. Groups were deliberately mixed in relation to the district from which people came and the specialities in which they worked. The nursing officers then split into three groups. One studied the job description of the ward sister or charge nurse, the second group the nursing officer and the third the senior nursing officer's work. They were asked to consider charts (A) and (B) and mark up their findings.

The percentage of time spent on various jobs per week		
50%	=	18 hours 45 minutes
25%	=	9 hours 22½ minutes
20%	=	7½ hours
5%	=	1 hour 52½ minutes

Chart (A)

KEY TASK ANALYSIS I				
Job				
Key Tasks	Time Allocation %	Difficulty	Importance	
				Chart (B)

Fascinating discussions revealed that some nursing officers had not been ward sisters or charge nurses and others had surprisingly little knowledge of the present job of their senior nursing officer. Amazing similarities occurred between the work of some nursing officers and the job of their senior nursing officer. This showed that there were grey areas which required clarification. At the end of the morning a leader from each group was selected to write up the group's findings on a flip-chart and three spokesmen presented the results to the class -showing ideas of the job as it was seen now - in terms of input. During lunch there were often valuable discussions and on day two, nursing officers - who had never previously worked closely together - were able to settle a long-standing disagreement over the treatment of a patient transferred from hospital to the community. The afternoon session concentrated on jobs as they should be in one year's time, that is to say in terms of output. Splitting into syndicate groups again, course members studied different jobs from those studied during the morning. Key tasks were discussed in terms of Planning, Organising, Staffing, Directing, Controlling - see Chart (D). Consideration was given to 'Time Span of Discretion'. A ward sister may think ahead, perhaps for hours, to plan her work, eg six cases going from a female surgical ward to theatre during the morning - or two months ahead as she organises the August holidays for her staff. The nursing officer however may be planning three years ahead if she is a member of the primary health care team building an ante-natal clinic in a new town. A senior nursing officer may plan a district hospital which will not be operative for 5-10 years.

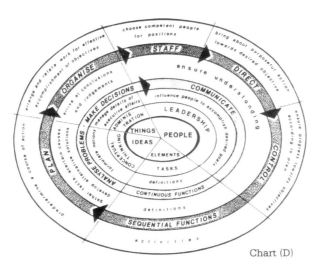

Chart (D)

After tea the syndicate groups produced a feed-back of their work and the flip-charts were all put round the wall for inspection. The work of the two-day module was typed out and each course member received a copy before returning home. People had had pre-course reading sent to them and further hand-outs distributed during the day.

Job improvement sheets, Chart (C) were distributed and each person was invited to think how he/she could make constructive suggestions where his/her own work could be improved, eg reducing costs, giving more job satisfaction and above all producing better patient care.

JOB IMPROVEMENT PLAN			
Key Tasks	Standard to be Achieved A. Achieved now B. To be achieved by ? date	Action necessary to achieve standard B. Who takes it, and date to be completed	Support required to achieve standard
			Chart (C)

After dinner a panel of speakers from areas, districts and divisional grades were invited, together with senior nursing officers. Running over sixty courses for nursing officers alone, we were able to draw on the expertise of nurses throughout the region. The evening panel provided a platform for people to voice their problems and disagreements with the philosophy of the course. Some sessions were extremely lively and valuable. With bated breath one mentions that panel members themselves appeared to learn a great deal and with each successive attendance became more fluent and free to express their ideas to the course. "The value of training courses is severely curtailed if staff return to an unresponsive atmosphere and unsympathetic superiors." (6)

The Second Day

After a welcome English breakfast the second day began with each course member quietly sitting down considering his or her own job improvement plan, Chart (C). This was an interesting exercise and afterwards all were asked to speak about their own items for 'key tasks'. One member was asked to time each speaker and many had to sit down when their three minutes were up! Each one was intensely interesting and each took back these new ideas to their senior nursing officers.

The next session was an interesting talk on planning. Lecturers were drawn from the nursing profession and produced many questions from one or other district.

The afternoon began with a nurse from area, district, division or a director of nurse education, speaking on the management role and organising developments in nursing. This was a time when much valuable practical information and advice was given. Evaluation forms were analysed and results were given out at the end of the afternoon. After each course we took to heart the comments and adjusted our work accordingly.

During the summer months syndicate work was carried out on the lawns under the azaleas and rhododendrons, but whatever the weather it was generally agreed that these two-day modules formed a good basis for the new appraisal forms recently issued by the DHSS. Previous course members are requesting help with their key tasks.

Summing Up

As a tutor to sixty courses I found each workshop rather like a meal to be cooked. Sometimes the mixture of people was like a successful omelette or a meringue - blending happily. On other occasions the workshop was rather like bread which rose too quickly or else did not rise at all.

Acknowledgements

It was a great privilege to run the courses and I would like to pay tribute to Mr W J Owens, Principal, South East Thames Regional Conference and Training Centre, and all staff who helped to organise and lecture; and I should like to thank Roger Silver, Regional Press and Public Relations Officer for helping me with this article.

Bibliography.

1. Reddin, W J (1970) *Management Effectiveness.* McGraw Hill Book Co., New York.

2. DHSS (1972) *Management Arrangements for the Reorganised National Health Service.* H M Stationery Office.

3. DHSS (1976) *The Priorities for Health and Personal Social Services in England.* Consultative Document H M Stationery Office.

4. (1976) *Sharing Resources for Health in England.* Report of the Resources Allocation Working Part. H M Stationery Office.

5. DHSS (1974) *Management, Education, Training in the National Health Service.*

6. Drucker, Peter F, (1970) *Managing for Results.* Management and marketing series, William Heinemann Ltd, London.

The workshops have proved so useful that there will be further courses in the autumn 1981/82 syllabus at David Salomons House, near Tunbridge Wells.

Footnote: *This pattern of training was carried out throughout the whole nursing hierarchy in this region. As I was especially concerned with the Nursing Officers, the article deals with this grade in detail.*

Management Development Workshop II: Change is Possible

ELIZABETH COXON TAYLOR, Senior Training Officer, Nursing, South East Thames Regional Health Authority.

The author feels that if just a few of the tasks put forward by Health Service staff in the Management Role Development Workshops were implemented throughout the country it would strengthen both morale and the financial situation of the Health Service.

One small but significant example of change was born out of the course itself and was of immediate benefit to a patient. Two nursing officers had been treating the patient from their separate standpoints - one in the hospital, the other in the community. They had never met, but rightly or wrongly they had blamed each other for poor handling of the case. Eventually they came together on the course and sat at the same table for lunch. They discovered their common interest in the patient, were able to review the situation more constructively and to strike up an understanding for the future. It was not a spectacular development in nurse-patient relationships but it was certainly important for them and for one individual patient.

Another illustration of change was produced during the feed-back by course members on the results of their key tasks. A nurse was able to show that by a scheme to initiate pre-packed trays for an Accident and Emergency department an annual saving of £3,000 could be achieved – there was no further use for a full-time night nurse whose job had been to prepare these trays - running up and down stairs every time a casualty was admitted. There appeared to be no reason why comparable savings could not be made in other hospitals throughout the country; and of course such savings, when multiplied, would run into many, many thousands of pounds.

Both examples - two of many emerging from the review of the workshops - highlight one of the essential attractions and advantages of such workshops; it is the benefit of staff coming together in an environment far removed from the pressures of routine daily work, interacting, exchanging ideas and opinions, freely expressing different points of view and developing new understanding of staff problems in a variety of specialities.

For some course members - for example the nurse tutors who were attending the course - it was difficult to accept new concepts, but as the workshops progressed they themselves became agents for change.

They came to recognise the potential of their own influence within the Health Service for improvement, and if only a fraction of the objectives they set themselves were accomplished the benefits to the National Health Service could be enormous.

Resources do not follow an exact scientific evaluation to be made of the extent to which change can be introduced as a direct result of the workshops, or the dimension of the benefits they generate. But a clue to the benefits gained can be found in the feed-back on the tasks undertaken by course members and on their value, real or potential.

A broad picture of how various branches of the Health Service can or may benefit can be seen from examples in the following different spheres: -

The General Hospital

Reduce wastage of CSSD equipment
Provide hospital transport at weekends for staff in an isolated unit
Reduce number of accidents in unit
Convert a nurse's changing room into a recovery unit
Improve relationships between day and night staff
Arrange a night nurse bank
Encourage colleagues to use visual aids economically and effectively (tutorial staff)

Midwifery Services

Provide a flexible policy to prevent conflicting advice for post-natal mothers Research into methods of treating the umbilical cord
Reduce waiting time in ante-natal clinic
Encourage breast feeding

Mental Illness Hospitals

Create a psycho-geriatric day hospital
Establish routine team review for patients in long-stay wards
Develop a drug out-patients clinic

Services for the Mentally Handicapped

Set up a half-way home for the mentally handicapped patients in the community
Provide temporary relief for relatives of mentally handicapped patients in the community

Improve chiropody services to the elderly

Organise dressings procedures of patients moving from hospital to GPs' clinics Establish routine development tests in the under-5s

Obtain parking spaces for community staff carrying out treatment

These suggestions, mostly geared to improving patient care, represent just a distillation of the ideas of 700 nursing officers who took part in Workshops.

Appendix 6

Report On MRA Conference
Gatchina, St Petersburg, 25ᵗʰ May 1994

Having received two invitations to Russia from Irina Roganova - whom I met for the MRA conference in 1992 - I was privileged to go to Gatchina with Barbara Armstrong Clarke. Ken Rundell said it was dangerous to go alone (Mafia and other problems), and Barbara miraculously responded, and we had our diphtheria jabs. Helped by Paul Gunderson's letter, nevertheless apprehensive, we left Heathrow (British Airways) not knowing how we would get by bus and train the 35 kilometres from St Petersburg to Gatchina.

To our amazement we saw a large placard 'MRA Gatchina' at the airport, and I recognised Ken Rundell. Our relief at being driven by one of the sponsors Alekseev Evgeniy, though we could not communicate, was overwhelming. On reaching our room in the hotel attached to the Nuclear Institute (where our hostess's husband works) we found we had en-suite bathroom – the water varied from very hot to stone cold as the city curtailed all electricity some days.

Irina arrived as we struggled with the stove to make a cup of tea, and we were given the most wonderful welcome.

As the days went by, our MRA team foregathered. Heinz Kreig, an ex-Nazi who had fought against the Russians at St Petersburg; Margaret Othman Sundell, who arrived with Tertto Laarsonen from Finland; Monique Chavrand, who gave a brilliant piano concert; Gretel Trogg from Switzerland and Ettingen; the two Lobsteins from France (she is Russian and was wonderful with translations;

and of course, Bill Carey, who helped us all with his efforts to interpret our contributions at meetings. His wife Rosemary was a great comforting influence. Gun and Wolf Ulstad came from Norway, and Jerka Mila who had been with us all in Poland when Irina had brought her choir of thirty children from St Petersburg to Jaslo. He is from Sweden. Both men played the violin. Two Polish friends came too, Marzena Wecik (my hostess in Poland) and her friend, also Dr Zahn.

Before leaving England I had seen a telephone post in the shape of the Cross. I felt the responsibility for our visit was in God's hands. The conference was centred round music. The psalmist says "Sing aloud unto God our strength - make a joyful noise unto God. My guidance was 'Show us Thy mercy O Lord and grant us Thy salvation. All nations whom Thou hast made shall come and worship before Thee, O Lord. Thou art God alone. For our shield belongeth to the Lord. Blessed be the Lord for evermore."

The first day we spent the morning with the Head of the Department of Culture and the Vice Mayor. The ancient bus, especially laid on during the whole week, took us first to a historical museum, then to a historical lunch place. We saw early telephone sets using Morse. Pushkin had used the museum, which had been a Post House, from which he hired horses. We had an excellent guide who said the bodies of 20,000 children aged 9 - 16 years old were found there after the war - two wells were filled with bodies. "We hope it may never happen again," said the caretaker. Word went round for us to pray for Heinz, who was finding the whole visit very emotive.

Many people tried to give us information and I made notes, but as this is a report for the reader I shall only mention main points.

Gatchina has 90,000 inhabitants, with industries including meat, milk, shipping. Good medical care, hospitals and polyclinics. Education begins with pre-school crèches and kindergartens. Five vocational institutes and post-training colleges are also in the town. There are also several music schools, a cultural centre for amateur artists, an art school, and we were told "Young children are alive with life and vitality." There is a railway now, a magnificent park -Pushkin lived nearby and 1786 was a date often quoted. Some of his life stories were put into his books.

Our first lunch consisted of a cinnamon hot drink, cucumber, yoghurt, raw cabbage salad, then Russian soup with chunks of meat and potato (they are desperately short of meat, yet they often gave us two lots of (undiagnosed) meat dishes at a meal.)

When we returned to the cultural centre, a Concert was put on for us. One child played the harmonium, others the balalaika and percussion, ages 7/8 and 13/15. The latter performed a sophisticated ballroom dance. One child's accompanist was ill, so I was asked to play (Schumann).

Tea was offered, sans milk, pancakes, always pancakes, and red-currant jam, bread and cheese.

In the evening we were late for the opening (cloakroom facilities seemed always hidden away). The Vice Mayor, Irina and other dignitaries welcomed us, then all of us were filmed saying why we had come (as we had to do on several occasions). This was followed by a wonderful concert in another venue. I'm sure Dermot McKay would have loved to hear his translations of Margaret Othman Sundell's songs sung by Russian children in English - the sound was pure magic as I had done them in five English schools too. The musical children's opera which we had seen in Poland was performed (a couple's child was stolen by a witch), also a lovely song and dance with the children dressed as mushrooms.

Some of the Russian pianists performed brilliantly, and one concert had excellent harmonica orchestras. Most evenings we were given meals provided by sponsors - kiwi fruit or salads beautifully decorated - potato cottage pies with cauliflower (cold) - tea and cakes, meant we never went hungry. (Ken Rundell had left a lovely cherry cake with a welcoming card in our room the first day. On our arrival he had placed Russian newspapers (in English) for us to read also.

On 28th May we began serious discussions on MRA. Following Irina's programme, I was asked to show my slides of Caux, and Gretel Troog gave a commentary. Whilst going back to the hotel I began a discussion with Gustatis Veronica and we had a deep talk - she is divorced with two children.

Dermot McKay and Tony Sursham in Cambridge

I took Irene Laure's video in Russian but the colour was poor owing to inadequate video facilities in Russia.

(Two days with no hot water or electricity in the hotel)

On the Sunday, a visit to the Library was organised and we learned that all new books on subjects such as ideology are very welcome. An artist showed her Ex Libris illustrations and we were able to buy some for friends at home.

The visit to the school of 1,800 children and 110 teachers was of interest to my own local school committee. The Head spoke of their present examinations and that 100 per cent were going on to higher education. Again I took many notes, but of particular interest was Heinz Kreig's comment on parents in East Germany not being respected by their children because they had not told the truth during the communist regime. There is no literature on how to bridge the two ideologies. The Head says he has to rewrite all his history lessons.

During the morning on Sunday we had an unscheduled stop at a Cathedral, full of worshippers, and then went on to another concert of instrumental music (using the original Russian drums and percussion as well as stringed instruments). The dances were beautiful but we were then encouraged to join in a type of Conga dance (the leader is a goat collecting lambs - I think - but great fun). I made notes of the steps for anyone interested! Irina gave me a tape of her choir whom I am keen to get to England. [They came a few years later and stayed in our village.]

After a massive dinner provided by one of the sponsors (who comes to Oxford this year) we were collected by my friend Veronica, who had waited all evening to take Jerka Mila, Barbara and myself to her friend's home for yet another meal. Veronica speaks good English and begged me for English books, so I have sent *Happy Families*, *The Boy on the Bus*, and *Coco the Street Boy*.

Our evening was spent in the home of Veronica's teaching colleagues, with husbands and children. Barbara and I were put in a lift with a seven-year old child. All the electricity failed - panic - Barbara came to the rescue with a cigarette lighter - pressed the button - and lo and behold, we hadn't moved, and our friends outside burst out laughing.

The last two and a half days included sight-seeing in St Petersburg which is 300 years old on 26th May 2003, so there were celebrations the day we arrived. We were taken around the Gatchina Castle which is being restored - the floors are superb and the portraits are very interesting. Some of our friends played the harpsichord, violin and oboe. Spontaneously, Mr Wecik and Gretel began an 18th Century dance together - one of the things that made our time so special (as an ex-ballet dancer I appreciated the beautiful portraits of 18th Century dancers).

One evening after visiting museums, we were entertained by another sponsor at the Rotary Club of St Petersburg. Here we were given (yet again) caviar, smoked salmon, cold meat, hot meat, whilst all around were the banners from Rotary all over the world. Barbara spoke as a member of Brighton Inner Wheel. The beautifully restored chapel was not one of my successful photographs, I'm afraid.

We had throughout our time in St Petersburg, a wonderful translator Margarita Amalskaya, also a man whom the team were helping with his problems of alcoholism. He changed in front of our eyes day by day. We have left so many friends and we must continue to pray for them all.

Lunch on two days at St Petersburg was at The Society for Open Christianity - a religious philosophical Society based at St Petersburg.

Clockwise from top left: Barbara's white boots;
Peter-Paul Cathedral; multi-national team; palaces;
delivering Bibles, with a hand-painted building behind

Clockwise from top left: Bronze horseman; Peter the Great; prison, with guide whose grandparents were inmates; the Conga dance

Our bus took us the famous 8-mile long road through St Petersburg so we could see many superb buildings and the lay-out of the city. It is like Venice with water everywhere (it is built on 44 islands). Bridges have magnificent statues. Palaces of yellow ochre, vivid blue, green, red, and the cathedrals whose cupulas are gold, green, blue and mixed colours.

On our first visit to the Society for Open Christianity, we learnt of their financial problems. The Theological College is thread-bare and unbelievably badly equipped. The St Petersburg Council is demanding millions of roubles to paint the front of the building in time for the Goodwill Games this autumn.

Ken Rundell's son lives in a flat at the top of the building and is an artist. We were told that the paint being used at present only lasts about a year.

I wrote this during the worst thunderstorm I've experienced in Britain, with a thunderbolt clap. Fortunately my phone, TV and electricity seem OK.

The Society for Open Christianity has as its main purpose the establishment of dialogue with atheists. Many outside the Church are deeply interested in religious questions. In Russia, too many believers simply dismiss questions and doubts of non believers. Believers should recognise that those who reject Christianity do so because they have not found the answers they are looking for. "This is not just a Russian issue but a global one" - quote from the Chairman, Konstantin Ivanov. The Society was started 1971-72. The director gave up teaching at the University. Prominent people noted that he was a Christian, and he was fired (my poor hearing, plus translation problems, I may be mistaken). His best friend, a pupil of Stalin, was exiled - some friends are still alive. The problem is the future - human rights, inability to speak, the tragedy of a church (Orthodox) trying to survive. "We pray," he said, "one day Yeltsin will change." There are cultural questions. The movement was organised in 1981 – people who believe in Christ - that they may be able to turn to the church - those who want to join a Faith. The Society is for all forms of higher education; it has grown from 130- 200 - the teaching is by people stressing Christian teaching and the Bible. For ten years it has been a school and theological institution - Catholics, Orthodox, Protestant, Ancient and Modern, staffed by University folk and Catholic priests.

In Russia, concentration is on the New Testament because it is easy for the young to understand. Conferences and meetings are held in the building and they welcome any assistance or support. Their idea is that Christianity is for everyone but it is difficult to open anything. "People are closed inside," he said. Before, the Russian thought first of the individual - then the economic problems and their difficult life with more cruel leadership. "You," he said to us, "bring softness like balm on a wound. You show how to live openly; each time I meet you, I thank you for sharing and for friendliness. We feel God is on our side together. We have too many problems, we have international conferences for teachers and no text books - it is a dangerous situation. We need 40,000 copies."

Large notices about Scientology are prominent in Russia. Religion is a dangerous thing- the commune relationship is widespread. There is a growth of Islam. It is difficult. There are not enough forces to deal with the problems. Salary twenty pounds a month. The American sects are infiltrating, especially on TV, because they have the money to pay and the Orthodox has not. The choice for many is a sect religion or none.

When many of the team had left, the remnants had to be interviewed for an hour on local radio.

Philip Boobyer (now a lecturer in history at the University of Kent) said we should not mention God or miracles before I left England, so when asked on radio why I had come, I said at the age of 75 I had been invited, and found the value of listening to the Inner Voice of Conscience. I tried to live by the principles of Absolute Honesty, Purity, Unselfishness, Love. At that, the interviewer held the microphone and said, "You mean the Bible."

The Gatchina Nuclear Science Director had coffee and spent an hour with us. He greeted us with the words, "It was God who brought you here just at this time."

The last day Irina's boss - a typical Russian, somewhat fierce individual, joined us in the hotel - she had initially been using our visit for her own kudos but we really tried to love her and care for her. The men drifted away, and six of us women were left. She broke down weeping, telling us that her mother had died recently and obviously she had not been able to grieve. It might have been the dining room in Caux. The occasion was led by the Holy Spirit.

On the bus one evening someone asked our interpreter what she thought was needed for her country. (The roads were appalling - every mile or so a car was either burnt or in the ditch having a tyre replaced, or generally out of action. We never exceeded 30 - 40 m.p.h.) The reply Rita (Amalskaya) gave us was:

1. Hard work
2. Willingness to learn new ways
3. Honesty

The last official visit was to a local polyclinic run by one of our Sponsors - it was begun before the end of communism. They were ridiculed initially but now they have a thriving business and the dental department does its own false teeth and repairs to dental problems on the spot. (I have slides of this!)

To continue a description of some of the museums we visited, we must describe the magnificent Icons at the Russian Museum. Sadly, our guide was very slow so some of us rushed ahead so as not to miss rooms of magnificent portraits, statues and other beautiful things. It was difficult not to lose each other, but we clung to our splendid personal guide Marguerita. Barbara wore a bright red Mackintosh so I could not lose her in the crowd. I must mention Barbara's wonderful white boots, worn everywhere. One sole came apart the last day. It was impossible to get it repaired in Gatchina so, as she had a large roll of brown sticky tape, by 2.00 am I had bound her boot in a parcel-wise manner. Her friends' faces when they saw us at Heathrow were a study. I prayed all the week that with her problems of sight I would not take her back with a broken leg. The last evening Barbara insisted on doing up individually presents for people who had helped us, including everyone at the hotel. We were quite tired by the time we got into bed. (Most nights I put on most of my underclothes, plus jumpers, as I'd lent my bottle to one of the Norwegian team who had a cold).

Our visit to the Peter and Paul Fortress, Church and prison was conducted by a guide whose grand-parents had been inmates of the prison itself. They were then sent away, and their graves are unknown (the prison was closed in 1922).

The Cathedral had been visited the previous week by Prince Charles, and he saw where his relatives were buried. There was a strange statue of Peter the Great with a tiny head, and the memorial of the archway he put up so that people could worship him, but it had promptly fallen down. The pulpit is not used now - the people prefer a homily lower down in the church. The congregation stands throughout the service.

The prison showed us what solitary confinement was like. One woman went mad after a few days, believing the guard had raped her through the wall.

Undoubtedly the high point of our visit was the Hermitage. There three million items, one hundred and fifty rooms, one and a half million pictures, and it took eight years to build - a Baroque building known as the Winter Palace. It was re-built after the Great Fire. As we entered the Marble Hall, gilded with gold, the mid-day gun went off. A magnificent coach that would have needed eight horses to draw it was near the entrance. It had been restored with Marshall Aid.

Much had been collected by Catherine II. Many French emigrants were offered asylum from the French Revolution, so gave wonderful pictures, furniture and pottery. (There was one case with English china - a dinner service for 60 people.)

I found the EI Greco interesting after seeing the Toledo paintings I saw when on an International Midwives Conference. Other things included a magnificent peacock and garden made with jewels, similar to a swan in the Bowes Museum; the Greek statues which are superb; the Goya ; Titian (particularly his flower paintings and children's portraits); 19th century carpets; Church and religious pictures; Italian Renaissance, Van Dyke, Rubens (the famous Bacchus, the Gorgon); portraits of Rembrandt's first wife Flora, also his second wife finger-painted when he was going blind - so many treasures with wonderful gilded chandeliers - quite unbelievably beautiful.

The Fabergé Easter Eggs made for Royalty to give to each other were superb, and silver statues for decorating dinner tables. The enormous wine-cooler (bigger than Penshurst's) also. One very interesting room was the 1800 Throne Room which became the Parliament until 1905, when the 1st Revolution failed. The Marble Pillars and the Malachite Room - so much to see and remember.

One room was presented by Queen Victoria; the clock was stopped at the hour she visited the Museum.

At one time, the whole Palace and garden were a prison for the Tsarina in St Petersburg.

Dozens of picture of generals in Napoleon's Army filled both walls of a passage, and I remember so many beautiful things that we saw, not forgetting Tchaikovsky's grave, alongside many other famous Russian musicians.

It was a great privilege to see works of art that for 70 years or more had been unseen by most of the world, and we owe a debt of gratitude to everyone who helped to organise our visit. Our visit to Irina's home, where we met her husband and son, was a joy as she made a tape of her choir for us to bring back to England.

Additional Notes

Libraries in Gatchina. There are five in the town - a children's – a central branch and smaller branches, founded by Alexandra at the beginning of the 20th century. 20,000 people are on the Register. The majority of the books are serious and can be taken out. Academic books are available to students, doctors, pensioners and young teachers. They can be taken home free but there is a fine of five roubles a day if kept more than three months. Since Perestroika, books which are popular are those like *How to Succeed*, *How to Buy*. Ratepayers are registered. Foreign books are welcomed. (Solzhenitsyn is at Vladivostock and having a house built in Moscow).

Reference books are available - old editions of local history - the Catalogues Bibliography of writers - literary periodicals, including first editions of periodicals - are available. Previously banned editions of Solzhenitsyn were kept there. Open until 6.00 pm each day. Cheaper for pensioners! There are lovely sections on art and language. The teachers' college use it and it is open Saturday and Sunday. There is a room for Exhibitions, which are held every month.

The writers' circle is held once a week - about forty people discuss verse and stories, and the chairman is from St Petersburg. Some collectors meet there - e.g. stamps and post-card collectors. In June there will be a National History Exhibition. They have Xerox but no microfilm facilities.

The artist whose exhibition we saw 'Ex Libris' cannot make a living, but has met many foreigners and is appreciated in Germany, where a friend has organised an exhibition in a world needing art. This is thanks to MRA She does teaching, landscapes, portraits and graphic art, and has a 'second mother' in Germany where she has made many friends. The Ex Libris idea is a German tradition.

Our morning visit to the Centre of Culture (we were greeted with tea and cookies) – we were told old and young could come to meet and make friends. There were two choirs who meet to socialise and sing choral music. It is paid by the Mayor. Folklore is taught more. The choir master whom we met had been there 25 years. Folklore has not died. Family tradition is part of song. Every year there are folk lore festivals with TV support. June 5th, Pushkin's birthday, there is a national folk-lore festival. The choir master is also the Postmaster. On 10th May the folk-lore group went to Riga – the group is of any age, old and young, can join.

The dance steps and choreography were of great interest to me, as I am a trained ballet dance teacher, and had spent many years performing and teaching national, Greek and other dancing techniques.

The last day we visited the cemetery of actors and musicians; you have to pay to be buried here. We saw the graves of many famous actors and the graves of Tchaikovsky and Rimsky-Korsakov. We later had tea in Ken Rundell's son's flat.

To enlarge on our visit to the Polyclinic on our fast day, we learnt that when our sponsor friend left the State system they bought a building cheaply with second-hand equipment. Everyone laughed because they left a secure income and risked everything. Now, the State system is collapsing and they are on the Up, importing equipment which is very expensive. They are beginning to establish relations with the Municipal X-ray department. The problem is work. In spite of unemployment they are giving work to others - much of the equipment is second-hand, though some has to be imported and is very expensive. They cannot charge the full amount because people could not afford it. They are working to meet their costs. His wife says "When is your salary coming?"

Insurance pays for the old, young and unemployed. (They have a contact in Ettlingen). Six dentist chairs – they work two shifts. There are twelve dentists who work alternate days 9 am – 8 pm. The law says six-hour day. Private dentists in Germany work 7 am - 7 pm.

In the evening we went to see the Bronze Horseman - the Mars Garden - St Isaac's Cathedral with the marks of bombs still left to show the city never surrendered, though it was starved. That evening there was a magical sunset, and Irina brought us bananas and biscuits as we had had no food for some hours.

Further notes on our first day. One Russian lady told us much about the butterflies, the Rose Garden, and the 16-year-old Postmaster's daughter in the Museum. A visitor was ill and eloped with the daughter, having been cared for in the house. The father went to St Petersburg to bring her back but returned alone. He was grief-stricken. He died and was buried with his wife. One day a coach drew up and a handsome lady with three children asked for his grave. She realised how much she had hurt her father and wept at his grave-side. In those days, 20 horses were very expensive, and letters took two days to get to St Petersburg. Now it takes a week! "Thank God," said our guide, the time has come for foreigners to visit us."

We were shown many craft exhibitions, and past implements for farm and house.

The visit was something I shall never forget and we had the privilege of entertaining the friends we made then, back in our village in England. The choir of Gatchina sang in a number of venues including the Universities of Sussex and Oxford, and we formed lasting friendships.

Appendix 7

Christ's Hospital Carmen

CHRIST'S HOSPITAL, HERTFORD.

Speech Day, 1st June, 1935.

PROGRAMME.

1.   CHRIST'S HOSPITAL CARMEN.

Words by *Rev. Dr. W. Haig-Brown.*
(C.H. 1833-42).

Music by *Collingwood Banks.*
(C.H. 1869-1877).

Unum concentum tollite
   Læto, sodales, sono :
Et vota bona fundite
   Pro Christiana domo.

Ne noceat concordiæ
   Contentio proterva
Neu tabes obsit corpori
   Neu febrium caterva.

Nostra favete carmini,
   Amici, quotquot estis,
Quos cura tangit Hospiti
   Cæruleæque vestis.

Mores honesti suppetant
   Et utilis doctrina
Et litterarum gloria
   Et recta disciplina.

Ut per priora sæcula
   Sic tempus in futurum
Det fausta Deus omnia
   Et Ipsum adjuturum.

*Artes palæstræ floreant,
   Quæ per gratum laborem
Et robur addunt corpori
   Et robori decorem.

Sit indies felicior
Vigore domus verno
Et floreat, ut floruit,
Honore sempiterno.

*Verse specially composed by Dr. HAIG-BROWN for the Girls' School.

Christ's Hospital, Hertford

Christ's Hospital Band, Horsham

Kent and Canterbury Hospital League Motto:

DO YOUR DUTY, COME WHAT MAY